CW00686489

A sign of a great book of theology is whether its truth cuts you deep, so deep that you are inconvenienced enough to stop and pray. More than once, I put down this book mid-sentence in awe of all the beauty Christ has given me to behold. Sadly, we live in a Christian culture that has varnished the beauty of our Lord, either by its sentimentality or its divergence from orthodoxy. Too often looking at Jesus is like looking at a mirror at ourselves. But Sam Parkison clears away the uglification caked over our eyes like mud, equipping us with just the right pair of lenses so that we can see the radiance of the glory of God in the face of Jesus Christ. Parkison is like a modern-day Boethius, using the prose of poetry to make Christology shimmer as it should. Read this book! Like Mary you will cling to Jesus.

MATTHEW BARRETT
Professor of Christian Theology,
Midwestern Baptist Theological Seminary
Kansas City, Missouri

Theologians are often good at telling us about truth. Less often, they excel at showing us truth in all its splendor. Sam Parkison's wonderful work shows us how fundamental truths about who Jesus is and what he has done for us show him to be most beautiful. Apart from my reservations concerning the brief section on Christ's descent, Parkison's book is a truly marvelous guide to amazing realities concerning Christ and the gospel, which should leave you rejoicing and in awe. Both highly accessible and unabashedly deep, this is a must-have resource on the beauty of our Savior.

HARRISON PERKINS
Pastor, Oakland Hills Community Church (OPC)
Farmington Hills, Michigan

In this book Christology and beauty are wedded together the way they belong. While beauty may not be the first thing which comes to mind when Christian's think of Christ, Parkison convincingly shows how vital affirming the beauty of Christ is for both theology and the Christian life. Readers would do well to give this book a slow read and marvel at the beauty of the Lord.

Ronni Kurtz
Assistant Professor of Theology
Cedarville University
Cedarville, Ohio

Here is a learned exploration of the supreme beauty of Jesus in a Reformed key, at a register fit for the non-technical student of theology, and all aimed at devotion. Our guide wants to help us see that the Christ of classical theism is truly beautiful; but more than that, he wants to help us revel in His beauty: Parkison's work trains our taste so that we properly value what, or Whom, is objectively Beautiful.

James R. Wood
Assistant Professor of Religion and Theology
Redeemer University
Ancaster, Ontario

Page after page, I smiled from ear to ear. This is a Christian scholar with his hands raised in worship. Parkison manifestly loves Scripture, and the great tradition of worshiping voices, and above all, he himself adores and marvels at the God-man. Parkison models the 'continual state of delighted surprise' that he commends. This is theology at its best, fueling serious joy.

David Mathis
Senior Teacher and Executive Editor
Desiring God

You'll want to keep this book handy for frequent re-reads and read-aloud discussions with your family. Parkison writes about doctrine in a way that is accessible and deep, precise and gentle. *The Unvarnished Jesus* will serve as an antidote to spiritual lethargy and inspire anew your worship of our glorious Christ.

GLORIA FURMAN
Author, *Treasuring Christ When Your Hands Are Full*

In a world that doesn't recognize true Beauty, Parkison offers much needed corrective lenses, helping us savor the excellence of Christ. *The Unvarnished Jesus* is warm-hearted Christology, mining the riches of biblical truth and historical theology. The whole saving career of Christ is presented, from Incarnation to Ascension. Here is rich doctrine with a point: it will not only sharpen your mind but will also heighten your affections for the Lord.

JOHN FOLMAR
Senior Pastor, Evangelical Christian Church of Dubai
Dubai, United Arab Emirates

THE
UNVARNISHED
JESUS

THE BEAUTY
OF CHRIST
& HIS
UGLY RIVALS

SAMUEL G. PARKISON

CHRISTIAN
FOCUS

Unless otherwise noted, Scripture quotations are from *The Holy Bible, English Standard Version*, copyright © 2001 by Crossway Bibles, a publishing ministry of Good News Publishers. Used by permission. All rights reserved. ESV Text Edition: 2011.

Copyright © Samuel G. Parkison 2025

hardcover ISBN 978-1-5271-1222-3
ebook ISBN 978-1-5271-1263-6

10 9 8 7 6 5 4 3 2 1

Published in 2025
Christian Focus Publications Ltd,
Geanies House, Fearn, Ross-shire,
IV20 1TW, Scotland.

www.christianfocus.com

Cover artwork by Joel Whitson

Cover design by Pete Barnsley (CreativeHoot)

Printed and bound by Bell & Bain, Glasgow

All rights reserved. No part of this publication may be reproduced, stored in a retrieval system, or transmitted, in any form, by any means, electronic, mechanical, photocopying, recording or otherwise without the prior permission of the publisher or a licence permitting restricted copying. In the U.K. such licences are issued by the Copyright Licensing Agency, 4 Battlebridge Lane, London, SE1 2HX. www.cla.co.uk

For Shannon

My Lily

creaturely beauty par excellence

Contents

Acknowledgments x

Introduction
The Most Beautiful Man Ever to Exist 1

1. Divine Beauty
"Beauty is in the Eye of the Beholder" and Other Lies 9

2. The Incarnation
Jesus is More Beautiful Than You Think 31

3. The Hypostatic Union
You Might (Accidentally!) Believe in Heresy 55

4. The Atonement
A Misunderstood Doctrine 93

5. The Resurrection
Christ, the Cosmic Firstfruits 125

6. The Ascension
Christ, the Prophet-Priest-King 151

Conclusion 177

Recommended Resources 185
Glossary 187
Scripture Index 199
Subject Index 203

Acknowledgements

This book has been a long time coming. I initially began early drafts of its first chapters while I was completing my dissertation, which was subsequently revised and published as *Irresistible Beauty: Beholding Triune Glory in the Face of Jesus Christ* (Mentor, 2022). What I affirmed there in an academic context in theory—namely, the idea that Christ is the apex of divine revelation of *beauty*, and salvation comes by beholding his beauty by faith—I wanted to put into practice for a lay audience. The relevance of my doctoral research screamed for a book like this to be written: a chapter-by-chapter meditation on the beauty of Christ. But, at the time—around 2020 or 2021—I couldn't adequately focus on a PhD dissertation while also trying to write an introductory Christology for the lay-reader, so I put it on the backburner. Since then, I have steadily revisited this project, slowly working and reworking its material. In the midst of many other writing projects that have since arisen, it would be very easy to just leave this project alone; but giving attention to it has felt like a nagging, compulsive need. I really believed in this book and couldn't leave it alone.

I praise God for his timing, though, because had I published any of its earlier drafts, I would have been settling for weaker versions of it without knowing as much.

This book is dedicated to my wife, Shannon, and she really must be the first person I acknowledge here. I wrote this book with her in mind—she was my target audience; a mature Christian who isn't overly interested in pragmatic and basic "how-to" Christian-living books, nor overly interested in in-house academic debates and scholarly monographs. This is theology for the mature Christian who simply wants to revel in the depths of Christ's beauty; and this description fits my wife. Not only did Shannon serve this project by being my imagined audience while I wrote, she made it possible by the thousands of things she is and does as my wife and my best friend. Her patience with me as I obsess over projects like this is unearthly, and I praise God for her persistent love and support. I pray this book is a particular blessing to her, and that it might call her mind to the infinite loveliness of Christ.

I also want to thank Eric Zeller, the president of the institution at which I serve, the Gulf Theological Seminary. Eric has always been supportive of my writing ventures and has insisted on their relevance to our seminary ministry here in the Arabian Gulf—I recognize that having a seminary president who is supportive of his faculty prioritizing time to write and research is not to be taken for granted, and so he has my thanks. Lastly, I want to acknowledge the good people at Christian Focus. Willie MacKenzie took a chance on me when he agreed to publish *Irresistible Beauty*, a show of faith for which I am profoundly grateful. I am grateful also that he believed in this present work, and it seems fitting that Christian Focus should publish this book as something of a lay-level follow up to *Irresistible Beauty*. I also want to offer my thanks to my editor, Colin Fast, whose keen eye

and suggestions made this book much stronger. For example, it was Colin who suggested the sidebars throughout the book and the glossary in the back to help the reader with unfamiliar terminology. It would have never occurred to me to include these kinds of features, but now I cannot imagine this book without them.

Introduction

The Most Beautiful Man Ever to Exist

Too few people today consider Jesus to be beautiful. The deficit of admirers of the loveliness of Christ is not merely a phenomenon among unbelievers. Many Christians today would struggle to articulate how or why their unbelieving friends should consider Jesus not merely powerful or trustworthy or good but irreducibly *beautiful*. Should the average evangelical Christian today read a quote from a church father like Augustine or a Puritan like Samuel Rutherford about the loveliness of Christ, he might scratch his head and wonder at the affective and evocative descriptions. The reasons for this lamentable state of affairs are legion. Some Christians struggle to articulate the beauty of Christ because they struggle to articulate the beauty of *anything*. Such a struggle is downstream from a wider cultural situation that the late philosopher Roger Scruton called the "uglification of culture." If there is no such thing as objective beauty, and all that we are urged by our culture to call beautiful is patently ugly, it is understandable that we might struggle to describe the beauty of Christ. Another reason why Christians today fail to be moved by the beauty

of Christ, however, is that their idea of Christ is simply deficient. The Christology operative among some Christians today is impoverished compared to Christians of yesteryear. In other words, too many Christians today are missing out: they fail to see the beauty of Christ because the Christ they conceptualize is a diminished version of the Jesus revealed in Holy Scripture and proclaimed throughout Christianity's Great Tradition.

In the face of such threats, this book insists on making the startling claim: Jesus Christ is the most beautiful man ever to exist. How can I make such a declaration? The answer is two-pronged: one side theoretical, one side experiential. Theoretically, I know he is the most beautiful man to ever exist because he is no *mere* man. He is the God-man. The man in whom "the whole fullness of deity dwells bodily" (Col. 2:9). All that is in God is in the person of the Son—the Word—who "became flesh and dwelt among us" (John 1:14). And *beauty* is included in this "all" that is in God. God is not beautiful in the sense that beauty is some external characteristic that he happens to have, as if he could dispense of his beauty and still be God. He *is* ultimate Beauty. In this book, I will try to erect a structurally sound building, with architectural craftmanship and artistry to showcase and adorn the beauty of Jesus. But crucial to the integrity of the building is a strong foundation. It will do the reader no good if I construct an impressive edifice on sand. I believe the endeavor to do little more than stare at the beauty of Jesus is fully justified—we build upon stone. The rest of this book builds upon the foundation of the doctrine of God: I will argue here that beauty is an essential attribute of God. If this is the case, the God-man therefore *must* be the most beautiful man ever to exist.

What of my second "prong"—the experiential one? Simply put, I know Jesus to be the most beautiful man ever to exist because I've *experienced* him to be so. I believe that habitually gazing at Jesus through the Scriptures proves him to be the most beautiful man ever to exist. Gaze at any other human being long enough, and you will find sin. That is, you will find true *ugliness*. Not so with Jesus. If you stare at him—if you read his Scriptures and you fixate on his person and work—all you will find are reasons to admire him. All you will find are reasons to adore him.

This experiential "prong" is the purpose of this book. What you find here is an invitation to put my claim to the test. Chapter by chapter, I look at Jesus's person and work in consideration of his beauty. Chapter by chapter, I invite you to stare at this man, and see for yourself if he truly is the most beautiful man ever to exist.

Before I offer you a roadmap for the rest of this book, let me head off a potential misunderstanding (a point I will clarify throughout as well). It would be wrong automatically to associate the divine beauty we find in Christ with, how shall we say … *daintiness*. In other words, the beauty I invite readers to behold in Christ is not sentimental. I will go a step further and insist that the beauty we see in Christ is not even, strictly speaking, feminine—as glorious as feminine beauty is. Indeed, far be it from me to disparage true feminine beauty. Man and woman are made in the image of God, both reflecting his glory in *gendered* ways. Masculine virtue and feminine virtue overlap at many points, but they are beautifully distinct and complementary. In this way, the harmonious beauty of man and woman is paradigmatic of all creational beauty, which is (much to the chagrin of our age) irreducibly orderly and structured. And within this fabric of orderly creational beauty, the Word became flesh not as an

androgynous, genderless human. The Word became a man. This fact means that Christ exemplifies masculine virtue and thereby affirms and showcases feminine virtue as its fitting counterpoint.

My purpose in saying all of this is to avoid problematic ideas we tend to carry about beauty in general, and the beauty of Jesus in particular. One is the notion that beauty is the same as "girly." It isn't. Beauty is certainly a category big enough for "girliness" to fit within it (provided that it is girliness exemplified by a *girl*), but it is big enough also to encompass manly beauty. We live in a world in which people are increasingly uppity about "gender" talk, and in which the world of aesthetics and art do not prioritize *beauty*. Louis Markos describes this present state of affairs in this way:

> Thus in the name of the egalitarian idol (for that is what it is), beauty pageants are outlawed, fairy tales are distorted, femininity and masculinity are either denied or conflated, the canon is purged of anything that is deemed (by modern standards) to be racist, sexist, or homophobic, and Christians (who should know better) allow their syntax and rhetoric— not to mention their hymns and Bible translations—to be neutered and "uglified" through the use of gender-inclusive language ... equality no longer means what it meant to the virtuous pagans, to the writers of the Bible, to our own founding fathers ... but a dull and colorless sameness that, if it ever were achieved, would make the old Soviet Union look like a fairyland.[1]

If Markos is right (and I really think he is), then we should want nothing to do with the mistake of either associating beauty strictly with femininity, or of erasing the distinction between femininity and masculinity and calling beauty

---

1. Louis Markos, *Restoring Beauty: The Good, the True, and the Beautiful in the Writings of C.S. Lewis* (Downers Grove, IL: InterVarsity Press, 2010), p. 18.

a wash. Rather, we should embrace the complementarity of masculine and feminine expressions of beauty and acknowledge that Jesus Christ is a man. That evangelicals have an odd penchant for writing and singing praise songs whose lyrics could have been written by a pop artist for her boyfriend is a well-known cliché, but clichés *become* clichés for a reason. So, Christians who tire of this kind of thing should be relieved to know that emphasizing the beauty of Christ does not consign us to a "Jesus is my boyfriend" kind of sentimentality.

Another related bad idea about the beauty of Christ is the fatal assumption that it is *tame*. It isn't. Granted, a small flower is beautiful. So is the gentle music of a summer breeze softly breathing on windchimes. But standing on top of Mt. Everest and feeling small and vulnerable and terrified is *also* beautiful. So is the way the midwestern sky lights up with lightning, raging to the heavy-metal-like music of a thunderstorm. Beauty can put you at rest and calm your heart. But beauty can also cause you to fall on your face in fear and trembling, terrified and awestruck and moved with gratitude and overwhelmed by wonder at the thought of God's holiness and grace. All the shades of created beauty are beautiful by virtue of their participation in divine Beauty: the highs and the lows, the peaceful and the thrilling, the subtle and the startling. And it's *all* found in Jesus.

Which is simply to say, the claim that Jesus is the most beautiful man to ever exist is not to deny that he is a male and not a female, that he is Lord and not boyfriend, that he is masculine and strong and not effeminate, and that he is sovereignly free and not tame.

It would be wrong, however, to conclude that my description here implies that Jesus's beauty is the "beauty" of a lawless and angry biker who is rough around the edges.

The counterfeit Christs described above have duped so many because within them there is some truth: he really *is* "gentle and lowly" (Matt. 11:29); he really *does* invite "the little children" to come to him (Matt. 19:14); he really *does* weep at his friend's tomb (John 11:35). We would do no one any favors by swinging the pendulum of our conception of Christ from one extreme to another; Christ is no more the cold, crass, angry macho-man than he is the effeminate pushover. His arms are to be greatly desired by his flock, and greatly feared by his enemies. His embrace is to be sought after as rapture for the souls of his disciples, and dreaded as impending judgment for those who rage against him. And the invitation to receive him as a delight, as opposed to a danger, is to be extended from sea to sea: anyone can get in on his gentle and lowly kindness. "Kiss the Son, lest he be angry, and you perish in the way, for his wrath is quickly kindled. *Blessed are all who take refuge in him*" (Ps. 2:12). So much for the caveats. Now, for the roadmap.

In chapter one, we will begin by laying down some theological foundation for the rest of the book. This will position us well to begin looking at Jesus directly in chapter two, in consideration of his arrival. In the incarnation, Jesus reveals God—Beauty himself—to us. In chapter three, we will examine his earthly ministry in consideration of his beautiful obedience. Then, in chapter four, we will continue focusing on his earthly ministry, considering the beauty of his sacrificial death on the cross. In chapter five, the beautiful sunrise of his resurrection will occupy our attention. Chapter six will focus on the beauty of his intercessory work, as he sits at the right hand of the Father in his ascended state, awaiting his glorious return and the restoration of all things. Chapter after chapter, we will see what Holy Scripture teaches about various aspects of Christ's

person and work—from the incarnation and the hypostatic union of his two natures, to his atoning death on the cross and descent to the dead, to his victorious resurrection and ascension, and the promise of his glorious return—and, with the help of the greatest minds in the history of the Church, we will see how the unvarnished Jesus radiates with a beauty that renders all his rivals pitifully grotesque.

1

Divine Beauty

"Beauty is in the Eye of the Beholder" and Other Lies

I once found myself on a flight next to an elderly woman who was in transit to her beach house in Mexico. Two things became clear from our conversation over time: first, she was *in love* with the beautiful ocean-side sunsets that painted every evening with shades of orange and purple and pink. Second, she was not a Christian, and therefore didn't know the God whose signature brushstroke so often tantalized her. I've thought of her often, and if I could go back in time and ask her one question, I think it would be, *"Who do you thank for all that beauty?"*

Let that question linger. I will return to it later. The central proposition of this little book is fairly straightforward: Jesus Christ is the most beautiful man ever to exist. Most of what remains is an invitation to put this proposition to the test on the existential level: "Come and see, I dare you." In order to fully understand Christ's beauty, however, we must first establish the relationship between *beauty* and *God*.

Divine Beauty

In Psalm 27, David writes, "One thing have I asked of the LORD, that will I seek after: that I may dwell in the house of the LORD all the days of my life, to *gaze upon the beauty of the LORD* and to inquire in his temple." What is the beauty of the Lord and how does one gaze upon it? We can answer that question by getting at one of the biblical corollaries of the beauty of the Lord, and that is the *glory of the Lord.* According to Scripture, the glory of the Lord is something every human being has access to simply by being on this planet. "The heavens declare the glory of God" (Ps. 19:1). What does that mean? What is the "glory of God?"

The nineteenth-century Dutch theologian, Herman Bavinck (1854–1921), is helpful here. "Glory," for Bavinck, was not merely one of many attributes of God, it was the perfection of all his attributes: "The 'glory of the Lord' is the splendor of brilliance that is inseparably associated with all of God's attributes and his self-revelation in nature and grace, the glorious form in which he everywhere appears to his creatures."[1] The glory of God is his "splendor of brilliance"— God's *Godness* on display. In other words, when God reveals to us any one of his attributes, in so doing, he displays his *glory.* And his essential glory includes all of his attributes.

This is because God is simple. He is not simple in the sense that he is "easy to figure out." In fact, God's simplicity actually demands that he is the opposite of "easy to figure out,"—he is *incomprehensible.* When I say that God is simple, I mean that he is not comprised of parts. He is not the sum total of his attributes—one part power, one part knowledge,

---

1. Herman Bavinck, *Reformed Dogmatics Vol. 2: God and Creation,* ed. John Bolt, trans. John Vriend (Grand Rapids, MI: Baker Academic, 2003), p. 252.

one part holiness, one part love, etc. He has no sections or divisions. Whatever he is, he is entirely, to the max, always.

Now, as finite and complex people, we are bound to experience this simple God in various ways. *We* are the sum of *our* parts—we are a composite of body and soul—we change, we grow, we suffer. To be *creaturely* is to be mutable (i.e., changeable) and finite. Before my conversion to Christ, I was a "child of wrath, like the rest of mankind" (Eph. 2:3). I was the object of God's righteous justice and destined for punishment since I stood before him as a sin-ridden offense to his holiness. But now, I am "made alive together with Christ" and am "seated with him in the heavenly places" because of his "being rich in mercy" (Eph. 2:4-6). This, however, does *not* mean that God *de-activated* one attribute (i.e., holiness—which showed up as wrath toward my sin) and subsequently *activated* another (i.e., mercy). This is because his attributes are undivided—his holiness and mercy and justice and power and knowledge are not *extensions* from him or *tools* in his hand; *they are his very nature.*

There is no "essence of God" irrespective of certain attributes that he may or may not choose to use. God doesn't sit looking at his attributes, saying, "I think I'll use *this* one … no maybe not, let's go with *this* one." God is not sometimes omniscient (i.e., all knowing) and then at other times omnipotent (i.e., all powerful); he is always omnisciently omnipotent, and omnipotently omniscient. He does not *have* love and holiness; he *is* lovingly holy, and his holiness is loving (and lovely, as we'll see). So, when I was an object of his wrath, I was an object of the God who eternally burns with maximal grace and mercy and holiness, with no variation or change or diminishment. My change from wrath to grace was a real change, but *I'm* the one who

changed. He was, is, and always will be himself—purely God from everlasting to everlasting.

In order for us to experience this kind of Being at all—the kind that is altogether unlike us—he must *reveal* his glory to us; he must accommodate his infinite attributes to us in finite ways. We don't experience God directly, but rather always through his mediation of revelation. Which means we don't experience his *Beauty* directly either. The first encounter we have with beauty is experiential on an earthly level—we begin where we are, and we know what beauty is because we experience its earthly forms. Incidentally, it is not accidental that Beauty is so notoriously hard to define. Beauty is intrinsic *to the object it adorns*, so it's unintelligible in the abstract. Beauty isn't a *thing*; it is a description—a characteristic. This doesn't mean, however, that beauty is subjective, and this point is important enough to dwell on at some length.

Sidebar 1.1
Omniscience / Omnipotence / Omnipresence

These "Omni's" affirm God's almightiness. Omniscience means that God is all-knowing, while omnipotence means that God is all-powerful, and omnipresence means that God is everywhere. These doctrines are a way of applying God's infinitude to the areas of knowledge, power, and space. God is not bound or limited in any way, whether by knowledge, power, space, time, or anything else.

Is Beauty in the Eye of the Beholder?

I want to emphasize this point because I think this is an area in which Christians have done very poorly in recent history. And our poor performance regarding beauty is *inconsistent* with the way we handle Beauty's transcendental partners— Truth and Goodness. Most Christians know that truth is

objective—most of us aren't postmodernists, and we don't accept the dictum that "you have your truth and I have mine." We recognize that a statement is true to the degree that it conforms to Truth. We also know that goodness is objective—most of us aren't moral relativists. We don't accept the dictum of "you do you," or "do whatever makes you happy," because we recognize that some things that make us happy are *objectively immoral*. There is a standard for goodness that stands outside of us, and an action is moral to the degree that it conforms to that standard. So, most Christians are *realists* when it comes to truth and goodness, but for some reason, when it comes to beauty, we embrace a total subjectivism. Even the most strident critic of self-expressive individualism in the realm of logic and ethics can find himself sounding like a postmodernist when he starts to talk about beauty. "Beauty is in the eye of the beholder," says he, without batting an eye. It just *rolls* off the tongue. I want to reject that way of thinking entirely. Beauty is objective, and to the degree that we see beauty in an object or thought or action, that object or thought or action is conforming to objective Beauty.

Consider our basic experience of beauty. When you see a beautiful painting or hear a beautiful song, the beauty does not originate in *you*. Beauty isn't found in the organ of perception (your eyes or your ears), nor in the sensation of perceiving (seeing or hearing). Beauty stands objectively outside of these surface-level categories and is the quality with which these categories interact. Beauty is *bigger* and *beyond* whatever object you've encountered that has awakened your enjoyment and desire—it *transcends* the confines of the thing you are experiencing. In other words, when you experience something beautiful, it is participating in the ultimate reality of Beauty.

Now, you may have never taken a philosophy class, but if you have—and if you paid attention—this should remind you of the ancient Greek philosopher, Plato. Plato insisted that, apart from and outside of the material world in which you and I live, there is a world of "forms" or "ideas." We see various trees on this planet, for example, but all of those trees are imperfect, shadowy participants in the *true form of treeness*—the Platonic ideal of the Perfect Tree—which exists in an immaterial world. Most theologians in the history of the Church—particularly following Augustine—have insisted that Plato is right to see a relationship between the beauty we experience and its Source, *but that he was wrong about the Source.* Earthly beauty is a revelation of true Beauty, but true Beauty isn't some abstract concept of *the ideal*, it is rather *God's splendor.* So, the tree reflects God's power—and thereby "declares his glory" (see Ps. 19:1).

This is why it is right to identify all three of these transcendentals (Truth, Goodness, and Beauty) as essentially *one*. That's one of the insights that Christianity rightly praised in the platonic tradition. The Platonists were right to see these transcendentals as one, even if they were ultimately unable to account for their unity. The ultimate True *is* the ultimate Good and Beauty. But in the hands of Christians, this conviction wasn't simply stated, it was positively *sung.* If the ultimate Source of all these transcendentals is found in the God who is simple, it should not surprise us at all to find goodness to be beautiful, and truth to be good and fitting and lovely, etc. All of our experiences with these realities are pointing us to God, because these transcendental realities are ultimately found in him. Beauty is recognized subjectively, but this does not mean that Beauty is itself subjective. So, our understanding of beauty begins *below*—when beauty thrusts itself upon us and we are compelled by it.

Our experience of beauty *begins* below, yes, but it mustn't stay there. The beauty we experience in creation has the purpose to direct our attention to the God who *is* Beauty. Again, the Platonists recognized this to a degree. They knew that all this earthly beauty was pointing *beyond* itself. They knew that the cosmos was enchanted—or, when they were at their most distraught by their existential blindness, they might say *haunted*. Reality *meant* more than it was. The referent of every earthly beauty was *more* than the material form that occasioned its recognition.

Sidebar 1.2
Platonism

Platonism is a school of philosophy that takes its name from the ancient philosopher, Plato (427–348 B.C.). Plato is well known for his "cave analogy," which illustrates his theory of Forms or Ideas. The Platonic tradition, which subsequently builds on Plato's own writings while further developing them, can be broadly described as philosophical Realism. Realism affirms that universal essences are real. For example, in Plato's case, there is such a thing as essential "treeness" or "dogness" or "humanness," while individual instantiations—trees, dogs, or you and me—participate in their transcendent Forms. Platonism was the primary school of philosophy the early Christians critically appropriated in the development of theology.

The early Christians recognized the angst of the philosophers—they saw in the philosophers' musings questions that they had the answers to, not because they were so much wiser than the philosophers, but because those answers were thrust upon them in dramatic fashion through divine revelation. The early Christians were able to answer questions the philosophers never even knew they had. The upshot of this is that, for the early Christians, the cosmos pulsates with life and meaning. Unlike for some of the

Greek philosophers, for the Christian, creation is good not *despite* its physical form, but precisely *as* physical. It is good because it is formed in the good mind of the all-good God. The material universe is not good *despite* its physical form; its physical form is *itself* good. But its physical form does not exhaust its essence. This view of creation is illustrated well by C.S. Lewis. He makes the point in a conversation between the Narnian star, Ramandu, and Eustace Scrubb in the fantasy classic *The Voyage of the Dawn Treader*:

> "In our world," said Eustace, "a star is a huge ball of flaming gas."
>
> "Even in your world, my son, that is not what a star is but only what it is made of."[2]

Christianity professes to give an account of what our beautiful creation *is*. Namely, it is a beautiful reflection of its beautiful Creator. "From below" beauty is beautiful by virtue of participating—in some kind of analogical way—in "from above" Beauty, who is God. And all this "from below" beauty is constantly harkening us upward to notice its Creator. Earthly beauty beckons us beyond itself to divine Beauty. So, where do we learn about this "from above" beauty—this divine Beauty? Where do we learn about God's glory which he displays through the creation that captivates us? If we heed the call of creation to investigate its divine Source, what infallible and sufficient witness might provide us with the details about creation's Creator that creation's witness itself might lack? Holy Scripture. If the final word on beauty doesn't rest on the Scriptures, it is incomplete—again our understanding of beauty begins "from below," but it cannot stay there. It's not *supposed* to stay there. It points us heavenward, to the God who reveals himself in Scripture.

---

2. C. S. Lewis, *The Voyage of the Dwan Treader*, rev. ed. (New York, NY: HarperCollins, 1994), p. 115.

When we let earthly beauty drive us to the Scriptures, we find even more answers to more questions. The Biblical story gives an account not only of earth's beauty as a manifestation of God's glory, it also gives an account for earth's calamity and corruption. The essence of all this ugliness is its *failure* to manifest God's glory. It is a privation from the wholeness of God's beautiful creation—a fundamental *lack* and *perversion* of the deepest reality of the beauty of Being. This is the other side of creation's coin that we've been looking at. Not only does Scripture tell us to see earth's beauty as a reflection of God's Beauty, it also tells us to see earth's calamity as *unconformity* to God's Beauty. Destruction and calamity aren't simply part of the same random collection of earthly facts sitting side by side with all the loveliness. Destruction and calamity are results from the fall of man (Gen 3; Rom 5:12-14; 8:19-22). The presence of corruption on earth shouldn't tempt us to imagine God as corrupt—the opposite is the case. Things are corrupt when they fail to manifest God's glory as they should. That's what *defines* their corruption.

Beauty and Taste

All of this, by the way, explains (in part) why there are so many disagreements about beauty. People have various tastes, and some insist that one thing is beautiful while others insist that the same thing is ugly. How do we explain these sharp differences? Well, we certainly don't explain them by saying: "It's a toss-up, beauty is relative; whatever floats your boat." I'm going to say something that is going to feel wrong to many of us (but it feels wrong because this relativistic way of thinking has become so pervasive that we don't even realize it's the air we breathe): *taste in beauty is not neutral. Some people have better taste than others.* It is possible for someone to consider that which is *objectively*

ugly to be beautiful, and that which is *objectively beautiful* to be ugly. It is, in other words, possible to value things inappropriately. Just like it is possible for a person to consider an objectively evil action—like abortion—to be a moral good, or for some person to consider things that are untrue as true. The common denominator in all of these errors is *the person.* That people can err in identifying the objective beauty of an object is no more reason for affirming aesthetic relativism than the fact that people can err in identifying the objective moral significance of abortion is reason for affirming moral relativism.

The good life—or, in philosophical jargon, the *summum bonum* (the "highest good")—is not the process of finding what you like *right now* and then getting it. The good life is the process of discovering what is *objectively good, true, and beautiful,* conforming oneself to it, and pursuing it. This is what the ancients called a virtuous person: someone who is *rightly arranged.* He thinks rightly, desires rightly, and feels rightly. His affections are rightly ordered. His tastes are appropriate. And he got that way through a *process*—he ever conforms his subjective self to the objective standards of Truth, Beauty, and Goodness. He doesn't simply conclude that some things are an "acquired taste," and then leave the issue alone. No, if an objective good is "an acquired taste," he considers it his obligation to *acquire a taste for it.*

Let me give you an example: when I was in high school, what I considered to be good entertainment was, I now recognize, pure trash. It was crass, base, and shallow. I could spend hours watching vile television shows and not see anything wrong with it. As I have matured, my taste in entertainment has changed, I believe, objectively for the better. I find myself less and less drawn to the ugly, and more and more drawn to the beautiful.

Now, it is important to remember that we are finite and limited, so some of our differences in taste are owing to the problem of immaturity or corruption—i.e., our tastes not being properly ordered—but not all. Some of our differences are owing to the limitations of our perspective—our *finitude*. For example, I may say—genuinely—my wife is the most beautiful woman on the planet. From my vantage point as her husband, I see aspects of her physical appearance, her personality, and her mind that others don't see. I can see more clearly than others just how uniquely she participates in the Good, the True, the Beautiful. I can see, because of my proximity to her, ways that she reflects the infinite Beauty of God that no one else will see because no one else will have the kind of proximity that I have to her. But some other husband of some other wife will, I am sure, say the same thing about *his* wife. Does that mean that beauty is subjective? I happen to think that my wife is beautiful, and he happens to think the same of his, and neither of us are right or wrong in an objective sense? Certainly not. The difference in taste here has everything to do with our limitations. The aspects of my wife's beauty that I *alone* see, which participate in and reflect divine Beauty, *are really there*. The aspects of our unnamed bride's beauty that her unnamed husband *alone* sees are *really there*. The capital 'B' Beauty in which our earthly wives' beauties participate and reflect is objective, but we are situated to see what we alone can see.

To give another example, I don't think it would be quite accurate for me to say that Romantic Comedies are, as a genre, wholesale *garbage*. But I *can* say (can't I?) that there is such a thing as "a garbage RomCom." Now, I may never be able to tell the difference between a good RomCom and a bad one, because I am limited and the priority of developing a taste for that genre is far lower than the many other tastes

I feel compelled to develop in this lifetime. But I can still recognize that those who *do* appreciate that genre can develop good or bad tastes within the genre itself. I couldn't say as much unless beauty were objective, and that a beautiful RomCom could therefore, in some sense, participate in objective Beauty.

Sidebar 1.3
Transcendentals: the True, the Good, and the Beautiful

This triad comes from the Platonic tradition. It affirms that at the ultimate level, absolute Being is the absolute True, Good, and Beautiful. Truth and Goodness and Beauty—in an ultimate sense—are one. Falsehood, for example, is not good nor beautiful. Evil is not beautiful or true, since ultimate Being is God's being, and he is the Good, etc. Christians have historically recognized that that this transcendental triad rings true, and is ultimately descriptive of God, who is the absolute True, Good, and Beautiful.

All that to say, conflicting tastes in beauty and art is sometimes owing simply to our finitude, sometimes to an immaturity of tastes, and sometimes to corruption, but it's certainly *not* owing to a definitional lack of aesthetic objectivity. Wherever there is beauty, there is a channel that is intended to draw us to divine Beauty. Which means, wherever there is beauty, there is a possibility to develop a more and more mature and fitting taste for it.

This much we know from a theological perspective as well. Consider your own story. When you were saved, it was because the Spirit of God removed the Satanic veil which prevented you from seeing the irresistible beauty of Christ. You were previously attracted to grotesque idols, thinking that which was ugly was lovely. But then the Spirit gave you eyes to see the Beauty of Christ, and you feasted on his beauty

with the "sight" of faith. And, as you continue to meditate on the image of Christ's beauty, you are conformed into his image from one degree of glory to another (2 Cor. 3:12–4:6). This is the whole Christian life: the process of losing a taste for sin and developing a stronger taste for Christ. And here's the point (to tie this aside back into our topic): all earthly beauty is intended to direct you toward this end. This very end. This *Christological* end. Earthly beauty is intended to direct you, preeminently, to *Christ's transforming beauty*

God the Trinity:
The Beauty For Which We Were Made

"The heavens declare the glory of God and the sky above proclaims his handiwork," says the psalmist (Ps. 19:1). Creation's beauty, in other words, is bragging on God. Day and night shout out, "Hey! See how beautiful we are? *God* made us; isn't he amazing?" On this passage, the fourth century church father, Gregory of Nyssa, writes:

> For we can hear as it were words teaching us: "O men, when ye gaze upon us and behold our beauty and magnitude, and this ceaseless revolution, with its well-ordered and harmonious motion, working in the same direction and in the same manner, turn your thoughts to Him Who presides over our system, and, by aid of the beauty which you see, imagine to yourselves the beauty of the invisible Archetype!"[3]

Recall the fellow-passenger I introduced you to at the beginning of this chapter. That interaction—with her obvious love for natural beauty and her ignorance of Divine Beauty—haunts me. I wonder how she would answer my

---

3. Gregory of Nyssa, "Against Eunomius," in Phillip Schaff and Henry Wace, *A Select Library of the Nicene and Post-Nicene Fathers of the Christian Church*, vol. 5, 2 (Grand Rapids, MI: Eerdmans, 1954), 5:272-273.

burning question: "Who do you *thank* for all that beauty?" Not knowing the God of the Bible, all she has to thank are day and night themselves. But if they could speak (or rather, if they could speak *English*, for they do speak the deep, ancient dialect their Creator taught them when he spoke them into existence), they would tell her, "Why are you thanking *us*? This is gross! Stop groveling at this sunset; we don't want your love. Our beauty is supposed to compel you to *do what we are doing*. Worship God, for his beauty enlivens ours!"

Beauty *par excellénce* is none other than God himself—the Triune God—Father, Son, and Spirit, distinct in persons, one in essence and *glory*. From God's glory all earthly glory extends. His beauty is the fountain; created beauty is the stream. His beauty is the substance; created beauty is its shadow. God is his attributes, one of which is beauty, which means God is necessarily beautiful. There is no standard of beauty that stands above God to which *he* must conform: he *is* the standard. God and creation don't happen to both be beautiful. Creation is beautiful because it was made by an essentially beautiful God, whose glory shines through his creative workmanship.

We see beauty in the natural world, or in art, or in language, or in human flourishing, and the purpose of the aesthetic quality of whatever we are considering is intended to lift our attention upward. The grand beauty of an ant-colony digging tunnels somewhere in the rainforest is intended to draw our attention *past* the ant colony to the ant colony's Creator. And we get access to knowledge of that Creator because he has disclosed himself to us; he has condescended to reveal himself specially to us (preeminently) through the Scriptures. But the process for considering beauty isn't quite complete at this point, because now we are intended to take what we've learned about this "from above" Source of

beauty and allow it to inform our understanding of the thing that drew our attention to him in the first place. The ant colony points us to God. We learn about God through Holy Scripture. We then look back at the ant colony with what we now know about God in order to understand the ant colony in a deeper way. And on and on we go. Repeating the process forever and ever, even into the glory of the New Heavens and Earth, because the beauty of creation points to the beauty of its Creator, and his beauty is inexhaustible. We never cease to find new expressions of God's artistry in his artwork because his artwork reveals his glory, which is eternal.

A common characteristic in virtually all conceptions of beauty is the element of *harmony*, which has a starting point. The harmony of all earthly beauty, as it turns out, is reflective of earthly beauty's Source: the Triune God. All of it reflects the Trinity, who is the overflowing source of all goodness and joy; the eternal one who is infinite, bound by nothing, limitless in wisdom and power, the standard and source of Beauty, maximally alive, and is pure unfiltered holy love and life. The One-in-Three who is an everlasting fire of white-hot holiness, burning in a perpetual and timelessly eternal *now*, never diminishing or changing or weakening or strengthening because he is already inconceivably perfect. God's grandeur is what grounds all creaturely grandeur.

The Divine Accommodation of Self-Revelation

Now, all of this "Trinity" talk calls our attention to a very important principle regarding theology: in God's work in nature and history, God (the infinite) is revealed to us (the finite) in finite ways. This means that God is no *less* than what he reveals in nature and human history (he truly reveals *himself*), but he is most certainly more. How could he not be? Were he exhaustively to reveal his infinitude to us, we would

have to be likewise infinite. How could a boundless ocean be exhausted by anything bound? This is what theologians mean when they say that the Scripture reveals God's nature *analogically*. In his work in history, the infinite Triune God reveals himself to finite creatures in finite ways. Of course, this does not mean that the infinite God is somehow bound or constrained by the creaturely revelation of himself, as if he is somehow in process with the rest of creation. From his timelessly eternal present, he reveals himself to time-bound creatures in ways they can understand. But if this glorious God demonstrates his essential beauty in creation, we should expect to find *reflections* of his splendor in creation itself. And the only way for him to reveal his infinite beauty in finite ways to finite creatures is to pile creation upon creation of finite beauty in gratuitous, multiform fashion. This is exactly what we find when we pause to ponder creation. Clyde Kilby, a personal friend and disciple of C.S. Lewis, elaborates:

> For the Christian, God is the supreme artist. It was He who brought form into the formless world at the beginning. We are told that God looked at His creation as it progressed and saw that it was good; when He had completed it, He saw that it was "very good." Since we say such things only of acts we have pleasure in, the Great Artist was evidently much pleased with His world. It was a world filled with wonderful objects, shapes, and movements, a world abundant in rich colors like those of the rainbow and the rose, rich textures like those of beaver fur and magnolia leaves, rich odors like those of the quince and the honeysuckle, rich sounds like those of thunder and running streams, and rich tastes like those of watermelon and chocolate.[4]

---

4. Clyde Kilby, *Christianity and Aesthetics* (Downers Grove, IL: Inter-Varsity Press, 1961), p. 18.

> *Sidebar 1.4*
> **Analogy**
>
> In theological jargon, "analogy" is used in a linguistic and a ontological sense (ontology is the branch of philosophy that deals with being—or, as a friend of mine puts it, it is the "business of isness"). Analogy conveys the idea of similarity—simultaneously appealing to likeness and unlikeness. Analogy can be illustrated by way of contrast with two different, related categories of speech and ontology: equivocism or equivocal language, and univocism or univocal language. If I say, "I used the bathroom at home so I don't need to use the bathroom here," "bathroom" functions univocally—there is a generally one-to-one correlation between what the word "bathroom" signifies in both uses. If, however, I say, "I'm going to take my bat to the attic to drive out the bat flying around up there," the word "bat" functions equivocally. The same word is describing two completely distinct ideas. But if I say, "I had a good cup of coffee with a good friend, and we had a good conversation," the word "goodness" in all these instances relates analogically. Their referents (coffee, friend, conversation) bear some analogical likeness, but also unlikeness, to one another. In theology, all of our language of God is analogical—my pastor is wise, and God is wise, but their wisdom differs not just in degree, but in kind. Likewise, "being" can be predicated of both creatures and the Creator, but God's being and creaturely being differ not just in degree (which would be true if "being" were predicated of God and creatures univocally), nor do they differ in every way (which would be true if "being" were predicated of God and creatures equivocally). Rather, creaturely being bears an analogical and dependent (and participatory) relation to God's being. Creaturely being is finite and ever-received—God's being is infinite and independent. Creaturely being is always from God, but God's being is not from another.

The point is that all of God's creative craftsmanship (seen in the created order, including both matter—which has been made—and natural laws—which have been written) has one marvelous consistent thread which runs throughout: harmony. How does a simple, beautiful God reveal pure actuality of glory to creatures that are *not* simple? How does

he reveal his infinite perfection to finite creatures who are complex and can only experience one thing at a time? He must *accommodate*. And he does this with a profuse and overabundant *plethora* of works! He reveals his infinite and simple glory to finite creatures by loading display upon display upon display of acts that showcase tiny fragments of his beauty. He places his creatures in a world that is teeming with life. He gives them bodies that feel the various sensations that accompany the seemingly endless different experiences to be had in life. Triune beauty is woven into the tapestry of the cosmos. Creation's harmonious beauty is a fitting, creaturely analogue to the God who is Trinity.

Sidebar 1.5
Accommodation

Since God is infinite and creatures are finite, God has accommodated himself to creatures in ways they can know and understand. In this way, all of God's self-revelation—in nature and in Holy Scripture—are a form of accommodation. God is never less than he reveals about himself, but is also always infinitely more. God therefore uses anthropomorphisms (human characteristics attributed to God) all throughout the Scriptures (i.e., Scripture describes him as having "nostrils" and "arms"). These descriptions are not to be taken in a literalistic way, but rather as illustrative forms of divine accommodation—he uses images and analogies and metaphors in order to describe the infinite in finite ways with finite words to finite people, since their understanding is finite.

When we wrestle with what God's Word reveals about the Trinity, we have to do so in a way that does justice to *all* of the ways Scripture speaks analogically about God, and not just a couple of verses. For example, the Spirit is named *Spirit* for a reason. In the Greek, Spirit is the same word for *breath* or *wind*. So, as John 3:1-21 shows us, there is something about the analogy of a person *breathing out air,* or *wind blowing*

through trees that fittingly corresponds to the Spirit eternally *proceeding* from the Father and Son. But that's not all the Scriptures say about the Spirit. If it were, we would be forced to think of the Spirit as an impersonal force like electricity. But taken all together, special revelation attests to none other than what the Nicene Creed affirms: one God, who eternally subsists as the unbegotten Father, who eternally generates the Son, and who with the Son eternally spirates the Spirit.

As we consider the totality of God's revelation, then— general and special, historical and natural—we see that God reveals his splendor through the harmonious splendor of creation and redemption, down to the beautiful, symmetrical arch of the gospel story: the Father sends the Son to accomplish redemption. Having done so, the Son ascends to the right hand of the Father to send the Spirit to take that redemption accomplished and *apply it* to God's elect. The story arch of the gospel is nothing if not lovely.

It is important to note, however, that in all of this differentiation we must not lose the central unity of the divine essence. Saying that the Father—not the Son, nor the Spirit—appears in Holy Scripture as he who primarily occupies the focal point of electing a people is not to say that he has a divine and electing will different from the Son's or Spirit's. One divine essence means one divine will. And one divine will means the operations of the Trinity are *inseparable*. Since God is one, God acts as one. The Son and Spirit's divine will *is* the Father's—the work of the gospel is the work of the *Trinity*. Another way to say this is that the divine act of the *Father sending,* the divine act of the *Son being sent,* and the divine act of the *Spirit being poured out,* are the one divine action of the Trinity. Everything God does, God does *as Trinity.* Everything God does is ever *from* the Father, *through* the Son, and *in* the Spirit.[5]

_____

5. For more on this concept of inseparable operations at an accessible

Granted, these are deep mysteries, but the point I'm trying to drive home is that the harmonious works of God in creation and redemption do not bespeak a crude kind of arrangement of agreement in the Godhead, as if the Trinity were a society of three distinct centers of consciousness whose unity is a unity of multiple *wills* (for that could lead to the heretical position known as tritheism). The gospel isn't some team effort, where three distinct divine *people,* with their own individual wills, decide to join forces to save humanity. Rather, the harmonious works of God in creation and redemption are reflections of the Trinity's eternal actuality of what theologians refer to as *processions* or *relations of origin*: the Father eternally begets the Son; the Son is eternally begotten by the Father; and the Spirit eternally proceeds from both. Thus, when this eternal and infinite God—who exists *in this way*—is revealed in the gospel, it's fitting for the one who eternally begets the Son to be the one who *sends* (the Father), for the one who is eternally begotten to be the one who *is sent* to take on human nature (the Son), and for the one who is eternally breathed out by the Father and Son to be the one who is *poured out* at Pentecost (the Spirit).[6] Everything God does is a revelation of God's inner and independent beauty.

---

level, see Matthew Barrett, *Simply Trinity: The Unmanipulated Father, Son, and Spirit* (Grand Rapids, MI: Baker Books, 2021), ch. 10, and Matthew Barrett, Ronni Kurtz, Samuel G. Parkison, and Joseph Lanier, *Proclaiming the Triune God: The Doctrine of the Trinity in the Life of the Church* (Nashville, TN: B&H Academic, 2024), ch. 6.

6. For anyone who is interested in this particular question, I do affirm the *pactum salutis*—or the Covenant of Redemption. That is, I do believe that the work of redemption is the fruit of an inter-trinitarian covenant, whereby the Father, Son, and Spirit agree to elect, redeem, seal, and glorify a Bride for Christ. But the *pactum salutis* is itself an *economic* category. The distinction I am making here is not the distinction between intra-trinitarian unity before the foundations of the

> **Sidebar 1.6**
> **Eternal Processions / Eternal Relations of Origin**
>
> This is a technical trinitarian category to name how the three persons of the Trinity relate to one another within the Godhead. That is, eternal processions are concerned with defining the persons of the Trinity in the Trinity's inner life—who God is in relation to himself, independent of creation or redemption. Thus, the Great Tradition of Christianity has historically affirmed that the one, simple divine nature has eternally subsisted in this way: as Father, Son, and Holy Spirit. The Father is eternally Unbegotten, the Son is eternally Begotten, and the Spirit is eternally spirated (or, breathed out). The Father eternally generates (or begets) the Son, and the Father and Son eternally breathe out the Spirit (though we should acknowledge that Eastern Orthodox traditions deny that the Spirit is breathed out by the Son, but rather affirms that the Spirit is eternally breathed out by the Father alone). These processions or relations of origin are eternal—that is, they do not begin or end.

God's Beauty: The Soul's Highest Calling

I said above that the good life is found in discovering what is *objectively Good*—the True, the Good, the Beautiful— and being ever conformed into that good. As Christians, we know that God is ultimate Truth, Goodness, and Beauty. Augustine was right when he prayed, "O Lord, thou hast made us for thyself, and our hearts are restless until they find their rest in thee."[7] We are made for God. He is the highest Good to whom we must devote ourselves—he is absolute Truth, absolute Goodness, absolute Beauty. And he has made himself known and accessible preeminently in the person and work of Jesus Christ. The Lord Jesus Christ is the access point, so to speak, to the ineffable glory of the

---

world and intra-trinitarian unity after the creation of the cosmos, but rather the difference between the immanent Trinity's unity of *essence*, and the economic Trinity's unity of will.

7. Augustine, *The Confessions*, I.1.

Trinity, wherefrom all truth, goodness, and beauty flow. As we worship him with our whole lives—with our thoughts and actions and affections all being part of the living sacrifice of praise we offer up to him (Rom. 12:1)—we will continually be rearranged and reshaped and rightly ordered. This is none other than the telos—the end, the purpose—of our souls.

* * *

God incomprehensible, we thank you for your gracious accommodation. We are creatures of the dust, unable to even cause our own hearts to pump blood, much less lay hold of your awesome ways. We marvel that you would stoop to reveal yourself to us. Since you are infinite in all your perfections, any finite description of you falls utterly short, yet you have chosen to describe yourself to us in such ways out of compassion for us in our limitations. Your self-revealed analogies are gifts befitting earth-dwellers like us. We dare not refuse the gifts you give us, so we gladly speak back to you the analogies you have given us. You are our rock, though you are spirit and have no body. You are our shield, though no arrows could ever approach you. You nourish us like a mother eagle, though you have no need to hunt, for you are the provider of all. From your nostrils puff smoke of wrath at unrighteousness, and from your mouth pours fire at sin. You protect us with your strong arm. You show us pity as our Father. You know our frame and remember that we are but dust. You are all these things—for you have told us so—and yet you are infinitely more, and what more can we say? We are beggars and borrowers. We speak your words back to you, think your thoughts after you. We praise you for your goodness, praise you for revealing your goodness to us, and praise you for giving us words to form our praise of you. You are the all-beautiful, and we see your beauty in the things that have been made. For all things are from and through and to you. All glory belongs to you forever and ever. Amen.

2

The Incarnation

Jesus is More Beautiful Than You Think

The night divine Beauty took on flesh may have been silent in *some* quarters. Somewhere in Bethlehem, someone was probably falling asleep. Somewhere in Bethlehem, all was probably *calm and bright*. But this night by no means enjoyed universal silence. Next door, an angry husband may have been yelling at his wife. And next door to *that* house a grandma—a beloved family matriarch—was perhaps taking her last breath while family sang her Psalms and mourners prepared to wail. Longing for resurrection. Somewhere in the region, a mother was probably telling her son a bedtime story, while another son from another mother was being mugged by robbers and bandits in a dark alley.

In the meantime, unnoticed and unnoticeable, a young woman labored in a stable. She may have been screaming (like how everyone imagines from depictions in movies). I'm inclined to picture her laboring like my wife labors: silent and focused, with low-toned groans to ride the contractions like waves. I can picture her brand-new husband frantically looking around the room for a place to put this baby when

he comes while his wife squeezes his hand. *I think it has to be that feeding trough.*

These things may have been happening the night Beauty took on flesh because he took on human flesh in a human world with human people doing very human things. Fighting and dying and singing and wailing and storytelling and mugging and sleeping didn't stop for the coming of the Son of God. The whole earth did not wait outside that little stall with bated breath in anticipation for the birth of heaven's Prince. The scandal of the incarnation is that it did not enjoy the company of fanfare. The Word who became flesh wasn't, initially, a shout. He was a whisper.

"Ah," you may say, "surely you've forgotten about the second chapter of Luke's gospel. The whole sky was lit up with heaven's hosts, announcing Christ's arrival to those shepherds. It sure didn't seem like a whisper to them (Luke 2:8-15)!" Yes, but that is precisely the point. They would object to this picture of smallness—this picture of a subversive entrance, ignorable and unimpressive. They would tell us of the blinding light of heaven, and the sound of myriads of angels with their otherworldly singing. Who are these people who insist something spectacular just occurred tonight? Does anyone remember their names? Nobody remembers these nobodies. They can make a ruckus all they want, no one cares, because the opinion of a smelly, lower-class shepherd doesn't stop the presses. The heavenly overkill of Luke 2:8-15 is divine irony. This, as we will see, is exactly the point. Beauty's whisper-like incarnation is altogether lovely.

We have established so far that all divine self-revelation is accommodation. For God to get any information about himself into our minds, he must stoop. And he stoops when he *speaks* through Scripture, which is "the living voice of God,

the letter of the omnipotent God to his creature."[1] But words in ink on paper is *not* his greatest act of accommodation. This infinite God stoops down and accommodates himself to a far greater degree when his Speech lives and breathes *and speaks*. "The Word became flesh, and dwelt among us" (John 1:14). The incarnation is the greatest act of divine revelation. "The incarnation," writes Bavinck, "is the central fact in special revelation, the fact that sheds light upon its whole domain."[2]

Revealing Who God Is

Before the incarnation, God revealed himself as the Creator God. He revealed himself as such *through* Creation itself (Ps. 19:1-6; Rom. 1:19-20), and he spoke authoritatively about his Creatorship through Scripture. As the Psalmist puts it,

> By the word of the LORD the heavens were made,
>   and by the breath of his mouth all their host.
> He gathers the waters of the sea as a heap;
>   he puts the deeps in storehouses.
> Let all the earth fear the LORD;
>   let all the inhabitants of the world stand in awe of him!
> For he spoke, and it came to be;
>   he commanded, and it stood firm. (Ps. 33:6-9)

This much is established before the incarnation. God is *Creator*. But in the incarnation, God deepens the story and expands our knowledge of his creatorship. In the incarnation, we learn that this Creator God is *Triune*. In Hebrews 1:1-3, we learn that the Lord of all Creation is none other than

---

1. Herman Bavinck, *Reformed Dogmatics Vol. 1: Prolegomena*, ed. John Bolt, trans. John Vriend (Grand Rapids, MI: Baker Academic, 2003), p. 385.

2. Bavinck, *RD*, 1:344.

Christ Jesus, the eternal Son of the Father, who is one with the Father and Spirit eternally. He *is* the exact imprint of the Father's nature—meaning, when you see him, you see the Father's nature: you see what the Father is—when you see Jesus, you see God.

We read in Genesis how God *spoke* the universe into being *out of nothing*, but then we learn from the incarnation that this creative agency is in fact a divine *person*. That was *the Son* bringing all of that everything out of nothing! The New Testament makes this point explicit in other places as well (Col. 1:15-17; John 1:1-3). The Son is the everlasting Word of God—the timeless Son of the Father, the Light of his Glory (Heb. 1:1). This is why the Nicene Creed speaks of the Son as "begotten of the Father before all worlds: God of God, Light of Light, Very God of Very God, begotten not made, being of one substance with the Father, by whom all things are made." Never was there a time that the Father was without his Son; never was there a time that God was without his power and wisdom (1 Cor. 1:28). The Son is he who is eternally generated by the Father. And because Christ is God of God—Light of Light—and because this God created the cosmos, there is no part of creation our eyes look on of which it cannot be said: "here, the Light of the Son is found." Thomas Aquinas puts the matter thusly:

> For as light is not only visible in itself, but through it all else can be seen, so the Word of God is not only light in himself, but he makes known all things that are known. For since a thing is made known and understood through its form, and all forms exist through the Word, who is the art full of living forms, the Word is light not only in himself, but as making known all things.[3]

---

3. Thomas Aquinas, *Commentary on the Gospel of John*, C.1.L.4.118.

Sidebar 2.1
Nicene Creed

The first iteration of the Nicene Creed was produced in 325, when Emperor Constantine (A.D. 272–337) called for a church council in order to resolve a theological controversy that was ravaging the church throughout the Roman Empire. This is known as the Arian controversy, named after a presbyter of Alexandria named Arius (A.D. 256–336) who taught that the Son was the greatest and first of God's creatures. The council concluded that Arius's teaching was heretical and produced a creed that affirmed the Son's equality of nature (*homoousia*—of the same substance) with the Father. In subsequent decades, the controversy intensified and multiplied to include not only concerns about the Son's relation to the Father, but also the Spirit's. So in 381, another council was convened in the city of Constantinople to resolve the issue, as well as to revise and expand the creed produced at Nicaea. This iteration of the creed—the Nicene-Constantinople Creed produced in 381—is what Christians most often refer to when they confess their affirmation of "the Nicene Creed." These two councils are known as the first two ecumenical councils of the early church.

How do we know this? How do we know that the Creator God is a Triune God, who exists in the three persons of Father, Son and Holy Spirit? How do we know that the creative power of the Father is a personal Word? We find all this out *when that personal Word puts flesh on and walks among us.* "And the Word became flesh and dwelt among us, and we have seen his glory, glory as of the only Son from the Father, full of grace and truth" (John 1:14). This is why Jesus can say to Philip with a straight face, "Whoever has seen me has seen the Father." (John 14:9) and why Paul can say that in the face of Jesus Christ we have "knowledge of the glory of God" (2 Cor. 4:6).

"In the fullness of time, God did not give us facts about himself," Fred Sanders reminds us, "but gave us himself in

the person of the Father who sent, the Son who was sent, and the Holy Spirit who was poured out. These events were accompanied by verbally inspired explanatory words; but the latter depend on the former."[4] In the incarnation, Jesus reveals to us *who God is*. He translates God into *human language and flesh and bones.*

Incredibly, since the second person of the Trinity is truly divine—that is, truly God, possessing the same glory as the Father and the Spirit—when he reveals *himself* to us in his human nature, he is, by his human nature, revealing the glory of the Trinity to us. Theologian Michael Allen sums the point up like this:

> The astounding thing is that the eternal Word by whom all things were created became a creature without ceasing to be that eternal Word, and therefore his very creatureliness constitutes the act of revelation and is the guarantee that revelation is here within creation and accessible to humans."[5]

Astounding, indeed! I invite you, then, to marvel with me at the grace of God. He has not left us to wonder what he is like. We are not stuck, without resources to cross the infinite chasm to reach our incomprehensible Creator. He has bridged the gap for us, in a way we could never dream up if we tried. He condescends far beyond stooping to talk to us in coos and lisps—he actually tabernacles among us.[6]

---

4. Fred Sanders, *The Triune God*, New Studies in Dogmatics (Grand Rapids, MI: Zondervan, 2016), p. 40.

5. Allen, "Knowledge of God" in Michael Allen and Scott R. Swain, eds., *Christian Dogmatics: Reformed Theology for the Church Catholic* (Grand Rapids, MI: Baker Academic, 2016), p. 17.

6. The word in John 1:14 translated as "*dwelled* among" means to "reside with" or "take up residency amongst," and it is the same word the Greek translation of the Old Testament uses to describe Yahweh's "dwelling" amongst his people in the Old Testament in his tabernacle (see Exod. 25:1-36; 2 Sam. 6:1-17). When John uses this word to describe

And in this act of accommodation—this act of supreme revelation we call *the incarnation*—the Triune God brings his inexpressible beauty into view.

Revealing What God Does

In the incarnation, Jesus reveals to us who God is *by* revealing to us *what God does* in the work of redemption. This is what the incarnation is: the Trinity acting to save a hopeless humanity. And at no point in this mission do the persons of the Trinity separate or act independently of one another. "This external act," Michael Allen reminds us, "takes Trinitarian form. The Son's incarnational manifestation before the world stage is not a solo performance. Though he is the only one who assumes human form and takes a human nature, he does so by the Spirit's power ... and the Father's will."[7] This is what theologians refer to when they use the term *inseparable operations*. The works of God are undivided because, as we saw in chapter one, God is simple. That is, he is not a compound of different parts cobbled together. This is important because it helps us conceptualize the works of the Trinity in a way that does justice to the united, single essence of God. The Trinity is not one part Father, one part Son, and one part Spirit, as if the Father, Son, and Spirit could just decide at any given moment to go their separate ways. Every act of God in the story of redemption is a Triune act. Once again, while from *our perspective in time*, it may occasionally appear as if the persons of the Trinity are acting independently from one another, they are, *from*

---

the Son's incarnation, he is appealing to a rich Old Testament image: Christ's humanity is Yahweh's new and permanent tabernacle—his dwelling place.

7. Michael Allen, *Grounded in Heaven: Recentering Christian Hope and Life on God* (Grand Rapids, MI: Eerdmans, 2018), p. 78.

God's eternal perspective, creaturely manifestations of the single divine will. Keep this in mind as we reflect on the different appropriated acts of the divine persons in the work of salvation. They appear distinct, but they are distinct *temporal* expressions of the single, undivided *eternal* will of the divine nature. The Son, not the Father nor the Spirit, died on the cross in a human nature. But the crucifixion was no less a Trinitarian act.

The whole shape of the gospel is inconceivable apart from a Triune arch from beginning to end. The Father sends the Son by the power of the Spirit to redeem his flock—to purchase a people for himself. He does this by living a perfect life on their behalf, dying as a sacrifice for the penalty of their sin, rising from the dead as a guarantee that his perfect life and sacrificial death are acceptable to the Father, ascending back to the right hand of the Father to intercede for his flock with his blood and to send the Holy Spirit supernaturally to apply all this work of redemption to his flock. All this is *why* the Son became incarnate. The Word became flesh to complete the Trinity's mission of redemption. "After making purification for sins, he sat down at the right hand of the Majesty on high" (Heb. 1:3). Why did he sit down? Because he was *done*. He had done with a single offering—the offering of himself—what the endless sacrifices of the Old Testament priests could never do: *he made actual purification for sins.*

Oh, let us marvel at the Triune beauty made visible by Jesus! The beauty, the fittingness, the symmetry of the Trinity's inseparable operation in the gospel confounds language for those who have eyes to see it. Were we who are lovers of Christ not compelled to cling to him in response to such lovely harmony? We were *drawn* by such beauty, were we not? God called us unto belief *effectually* (Rom. 8:28-30). And what made this effectual calling *effectual* is that we saw

in Christ and his work something desirable—something altogether *lovely*. That was the beauty of the Triune God we were responding to with adoring faith, whether we had the language to describe it as such or not.

Revealing Our Need

But it's not just the glorious action of the Trinity that Christ reveals to us in the incarnation. Notice the layered nature of God's revelation in the incarnation. God reveals things to us not simply in the *fact* of the incarnation, but indeed, he reveals much to us in the *manner* of the incarnation. Christ came to us in humility. He came *low*. So low, in fact, that you would have to stoop to receive him.

The entire event of the incarnation—from the beginning of Christ's life to his death on the cross—is marked by one example of degradation after another. The Son of God degrades himself. He, the God-man, is born to a young virgin in a small backwater town—his birth is the occasion for a lifetime of slander for Mary—the unmarried, teen mom (however primitive you insist first century Palestine was, you must remember that they knew *virgins don't get pregnant*). His first cradle is an animal's slop bucket—*that's* where the eternal Son of God sleeps for the first time in his human nature. Then, all of heaven came to announce the most important event in human history to men from one of the most despised classes in society (shepherds). People to whom no one would pay attention. Heaven designated the most obscure and insignificant people to serve as hype men for the Messiah.

But the humiliation doesn't stop there. In his life, God the Son chose country bumpkins and mobsters and hookers to be his followers during his earthly ministry. He then defeats Satan, sin, and death by dying on a cross, naked and shamed

like a common criminal. He's a conqueror who conquered by being conquered. And to top it off, the first witnesses of the resurrection are women, whose testimonies in that historical context were seen as useless, even in the court of law.

Now, why do I focus on the counterintuitive meekness of the gospel? Simply this: the incarnation reveals that our situation is dire. In his infinite wisdom, God contrived a gospel message that none of us could rightly embrace with a haughty attitude. We have to stoop down from our prideful self-sufficiency to lay all of our hopes on a Savior who was weak and fragile. The incarnation says to all of us: "That's how needy you are. You're so needy you need a slop-bucket Savior. Your sin is so wretched that you need the Son of God to become a human and die a gruesome death to atone for it. You are so doomed that the only way for God to turn aside his burning justice from you is to take it upon himself in the person and work of Jesus Christ. You are so hopeless at obeying God that God himself obeys for you in the person and work of Jesus Christ. You are so helpless to know and worship God, that the Son of God becomes one of you so that you might know and worship him that way. He stoops down to make himself available to you, because you are so unable to climb up to him."

The aesthetic appeal of this Savior is very earthy. The stuffy nobility of our world cannot appreciate what happens here. But for those who are low, the coming of the Son of God staggers. The loveliness of the degrading incarnation is captured well in a poem entitled, *Immanuel*, which reads:

> See the curiosity of the cosmos
> As the Christ condescends to His most cherished
> creatures
> See the astonishment of angels as the Almighty advances
> towards Earth
> See the humility of the pre-existing King born of a virgin
> birth

The Infinite becomes infant
The Maker becomes man
The divine becomes despised
And the Christ is crucified
The Author of all creation cursed upon the tree
That He himself spoke into being
And the Lord of life was laid in a tomb
But the grave could not contain Him
And so the Son of Man was raised to life.[8]

As long as we stand, head tall, giving every soul we meet a perfect view of our nostrils, a slop-bucket Savior will appear as nothing more than a sad and curious historical aberration. But for those of us that get down on our hands and knees, with the straw and dirt and cow-pies, what we find there is Beauty that defies language. We find there that God has dignified and beautified *everything*. This is a planet upon which the Son of God has walked in human flesh. Earth-dwellers can now say, "God became one of us," which means we can no longer call anything earthly "ordinary." Oxygen has been graced to flow into the lungs of the God-man.

If you could fish somewhere in the Mediterranean Sea, and if your fish could tell you its greatest claim to fame, it would tell you, no doubt, "In my family tree, *one of my distant relatives was eaten and digested by God-in-the-flesh, and then went up into heaven in his belly*." And nothing has been infused with as much beauty in the incarnation as the human race. Every fetus that has ever existed—whether miscarried, grown, or murdered—is, by virtue of existing as a human, in good (nay, the greatest) company. The most dignifying and beautifying thing God ever did for humanity was the Son's incarnation. "The Word became flesh." We can never go back. Beauty has made his irreversible mark on the earth.

---

8. Beautiful Eulogy, *Immanuel*, 2017.

Revealing Our Provision

In the incarnation, Christ reveals the severity of our lack by filling it with his sufficiency. He shows us how needy we are by meeting our needs. He is our Mediator, who stands between us and God. His role as Mediator works on several levels. In addition to his mediating our knowledge of God, Jesus mediates *peace with God*. "For there is one God, and there is one mediator between God and men, the man Christ Jesus, who gave himself as a ransom for all which is the testimony given at the proper time" (1 Tim. 2:5-7). This is his priestly work, whereby he stands as a representative of man before God, offering on our behalf his blood sacrifice to atone for our sins, and also the perfect worship and obedience we could never offer ourselves. He also stands as a representative of God before man, communicating exactly only what the Father communicates. He stands between us and God and secures reconciliation. His body, in other words, becomes the bridge that covers the chasm of our sin and God's wrath.[9] "For it was indeed fitting that we should have such a high priest, holy, innocent, unstained, separated from sinners, and exalted above the heavens. He has no need, like those high priests, to offer sacrifices daily, first for his own sins and then for those of the people, since he did this once for all when he offered up himself" (Heb. 7:26-27).

But it gets even better. Not only does Jesus meet our need by mediating peace with God, he also meets our need by mediating *our worship*. The fourth-century Church father, Athanasius, says this brilliantly:

> For since human beings, having rejected the contemplation of God and as though sunk in an abyss with their eyes held downwards, seeking God in creation and things perceptible,

---

9. We will have recourse to continue to develop these ideas in subsequent chapters.

setting up for themselves mortal humans and demons as gods, for this reason the lover of human beings and the common Savior of all, takes to himself a body and dwells as human among humans and draws to himself the perceptible senses of all human beings, so that those who think that God is in things corporeal might, from what the Lord wrought through the actions of the body, know the truth and through him might consider the Father.[10]

What's Athanasius saying? He's saying that God, recognizing our inability to lift our gaze up from the created order to heaven, came down from heaven to the created order to stand at our eye level. He's saying, "Since human beings couldn't seem to stop worshiping creation instead of the Creator, the Creator became a creature to accommodate their limitations!" Like a father who drops to his knee to gather the attention of his son mid-tantrum, God stoops to bring himself to our eye level. In this way, he becomes intelligible enough for us to worship him. We can identify this *human being*—Jesus Christ, the most beautiful human being ever to exist—as the central object of our worship and offer all of our praise to him without the fear of dishonoring God precisely because he is no *mere* human: he himself is God. He has become man in order to accommodate our limitations in worship. We couldn't reach up onto the top shelf to get God, so God places himself on the bottom shelf— right within our reach—in the person of Jesus Christ, the carpenter from Nazareth.

"Without Ceasing to Be God"

It is precisely at this point, however, that many well-meaning evangelicals go astray. For they often miss the very central

---

10. St. Athanasius the Great of Alexandria, *On the Incarnation*, trans. John Behr, (Yonkers, NY: St Vladimir's Seminary Press, 2014), Ch 15.2.

point that while, in the incarnation, God the Son brings himself down to the bottom shelf in *one* sense, there is *another* sense in which he stays right where he is. Every Christian agrees that the incarnation—with its doctrinal emphasis on Christ's *two natures*, one human and one divine, united in *one person*—is one of Christianity's central mysteries. But often, this mystery is neglected for the sake of rhetorical convenience. "Christ was so generous he *left behind his divine* attributes," is how this point typically appears. And to be fair, it sounds attractive on the surface. Isn't this how Christ "sympathizes with our weaknesses" (Heb. 4:15)? Doesn't he sympathize with our weakness by *giving up* his divine strength? As shocking as it may sound, we must say *no*.

Some might object with a very important section of Scripture that *appears* to make the very point I intend to reject, however. This passage is Philippians 2:4-8, which says, among other things, that Christ, "though he was in the form of God, did not count equality with God a thing to be grasped, but *emptied himself*, by taking on the form of a servant, being born in likeness of men. And being found in human form, he humbled himself by becoming obedient to the point of death, even death on a cross." There you have it! What else could his "self-emptying" mean but a relinquishing of his divine attributes or divine prerogatives? But the issue is not as simple as that. For one thing, the central phrase of this passage does not provide its own direct object. Christ "empties himself" … *of what?* To assume that the answer to this question is, "his divine attributes," or "his divine prerogatives," is a bridge too far. The passage simply doesn't make that point. Instead, we see a grammatical tangle, that very intentionally keeps Christ "*in the form of God*"—wherein he "did not need to grasp for equality with

God" because he already had it—and yet, while *being* in the form of God, he "self-empties." Paul is very careful with his language precisely to bring us to the very limitations of language itself.

Again, we would expect this verb "self-empties" to have a direct object explicitly stated. Instead, we have to look for the direct object from within the context, and the direct object turns out to be a grammatical paradox—which is fitting, given how mysterious the incarnation is. Christ empties himself, *not by giving anything up*, but specifically by *"taking on the form of a servant."* The way Christ "empties himself" is not actually by *getting rid of anything*—how *our* self-emptying would necessarily work—rather, Christ "empties himself" precisely by himself *assuming* a human nature: his "self-emptying" is a subtraction by assumption—a subtraction *that isn't really a subtraction*!

So, no, Philippians 2:4-8 (and other similar passages) do not teach us that Christ leaves his divine attributes behind when he assumes a human nature. But we can and must reject such a notion not only because it isn't taught in Scripture, but also because it *contradicts* important doctrines that *are* taught in Scripture. Let me conclude this section with two reasons for rejecting the idea that Christ gave up any part of his divine nature or glory in the incarnation.

First, to say that Christ "gives up his divinity" or "gives up his divine attributes" (or even *some of them*) in the incarnation is to misunderstand the *hypostatic union* (i.e., the doctrine that describes how the divine nature and human nature are united in the *Person*, Jesus Christ). The statement on Christology from Chalcedon, which was produced by the fifth-century Church Council, in what is now modern day Turkey in A.D. 451, emphasizes the hypostatic union by describing how Christ is "truly God and truly man." It goes

on to say that Christ is "consubstantial with us *according to manhood*," and "begotten before all ages of the Father *according to the Godhead*." Lest we think that the church fathers at Chalcedon were teaching two Christs—as if there was a *man* Christ, and a *divine* Christ—they go on to confess "one and the Same Christ, Son, Lord, Only-begotten,"—and here's where it gets interesting—"to be acknowledged in two natures, *without confusion, without change, without division, without separation;* the distinction of the natures being by no means taken away by the union, but rather the property of each nature being preserved, and concurring in one Person and one Subsistence, not parted or divided into two persons, but one and the same Son."[11]

Now, I know that's a mouthful, but it's very important we get this right. There are not two Christs, one divine and one human. And at the same time, it is not as if Christ is *trading one nature for another*, which is how we treat the incarnation when we describe it as Christ "leaving behind" (at least part of) his divine nature or status or prerogative. Rather, "each nature" is "preserved … inconfusedly." The theological phrase that describes this point precisely is "the communication of idioms" (or, if you like in the Latin, *communicatio idiomatum*). This concept simply means that whatever we can say about either of Christ's natures, we can say truly about the *person* of Christ, but not everything we can say about one of Christ's natures can we say about the other. For example, can we say that *God the Son* died on the cross? We'd better! The one *person*—who exists in two natures—died on the cross. But can we say that Christ's *divine nature* died on the cross? We'd better not! Jesus Christ,

---

11. "The Chalcedonian Definition" in Chad Van Dixhoorn, *Creeds, Confessions, and Catechisms: A Reader's Edition* (Wheaton, IL: Crossway, 2022), p. 27.

who has a divine nature, *truly died*, but not according to his divine nature. When some say that Christ "gives up" part of his divine nature or divine attributes in the incarnation, they are confusing his two distinct natures. That's the first reason we should reject such a conception.[12]

Sidebar 2.2
Kenoticism

Kenoticism describes a theological school of thought that arose in the nineteenth century and has persisted ever since. Kenoticism takes its name from the Greek word, *kenosis*, meaning to "self-empty," which is the word Paul uses in Philippians 2:7 to describe the Son's "taking on the form of a servant." Kenoticism can be broadly described as a spectrum of views—all of which are historically aberrant—that describe Christ's "self-emptying" as some kind of metaphysical divestment of something divine. Strong kenoticism teaches that Christ empties himself of the divine nature entirely in the incarnation, while weak—or functional—kenoticism teaches that Christ empties himself of divine prerogatives and privileges. All forms of kenoticism are erroneous, since they misunderstand how the two natures of Christ relate (and since they read into Philippians 2:7 theological implications that Paul did not intend).

Second, if we say that Christ "gave up" his divine attributes or prerogatives, we actually undermine the gospel itself. To make such an assertion is to strip the incarnation of its benefits. I know this is a stark claim, but hear me out. If the point I've been trying to make throughout this entire chapter is true, and Christ *reveals* the divine nature to us in the incarnation, how could he do that if he "leaves behind" his divine nature or divine attributes in the incarnation? In 2 Corinthians 8:9, Paul says that Christ "was rich, yet for your sake he became poor, so that you by his poverty may become rich." Now, if this means that his "self-impoverishment" amounts to him

---

12. More on all these points in the following chapter.

"*forsaking his heavenly* riches," what riches are left to offer us in salvation? No, rather, this point from 2 Corinthians 8:9 is making the same point of Philippians 2:7—Christ's "poverty" and "self-emptying" amount to the assumption of his human nature. They don't constitute the renunciation of his divine attributes or divine nature. If they did, he couldn't show us the glory of the Trinity—because he can't show us what he has left behind—he couldn't make us rich *in himself*—he can't enrich us with what he no longer has. This is the mystery of the incarnation: Christ, without ceasing to be God, became man, so that in him, we might become reunited to God. Christ, without ceasing to be rich, became poor, so that in his poverty, we might become rich.

This is all a way of affirming a very important doctrine with a very unfortunate name: the *extra calvinisticum*. It's named after John Calvin, and it is unfortunately named because John Calvin didn't come up with it. To Calvin's credit, he did express it in a very lovely way: "The Son of God descended miraculously from heaven, yet without abandoning heaven; was pleased to be conceived miraculously in the Virgin's womb, to live on the earth, and hang upon the cross, and yet always filled the world as from the beginning."[13] But over a millennium before Calvin wrote those beautiful words, the fourth-century church father, Athanasius, wrote this:

> For he was not enclosed in the body, nor was he in the body but not elsewhere. Nor while he moved that [body] was the universe left void of his activity and providence. But, what is most marvelous, being the Word, he was not contained by anyone, but rather himself contained everything. And, as being in all creation, he is in essence outside of everything by his own power, arranging everything and unfolding

---

13. John Calvin, *Institutes of the Christian Religion* (Peabody, MA: Hendrickson Publishers, 2008), 2.13.4.

his own providence in everything to all things, and giving life to each thing and to all things together, containing the universe and not being contained, but being wholly, in every respect, in his own Father alone. So also, being in the human body, and himself giving it life, he properly gives life to the universe also, and was both in everything and outside of all.[14]

This seems to be a necessary implication from various New Testament passages. For example, in Colossians 1:15-18 and Hebrews 1:1-3, the Son of God is credited not only for the origin of the created universe but also its continual maintenance ("... and in him all things hold together," Col. 1:17b; "... and he upholds the universe by the word of his power," Heb. 1:3). If this is true at *any* point of creation's existence, it is true for every point, including those days in which the earth enjoyed the physical presence of Jesus Christ of Nazareth. To be the cosmos is to be upheld by the eternal Son of God. I know I may be overly redundant here, but let me try to make the point by posing and answering three questions:

Question 1: "Who upheld the cosmos before the incarnation?"

Question 2: "Who upheld the cosmos *during Christ's earthly pilgrimage* two thousand years ago?"

Question 3: "Who upholds the cosmos *right now*?"

Astonishingly, the answer to all three of those questions is exactly the same: God the *Son*. Jesus upheld the cosmos before, during, and after the incarnation in his divine nature. The one Triune God—who subsists eternally as Father, Son, and Holy Spirit—wills and acts and operates inseparably as one God. There is no exception to this rule, even during the

---

14. Athanasius, *On the Incarnation*. Ch 15.2.

incarnation, which means the beautiful human who dwells among us in the incarnation reveals divine Beauty to us precisely because he *is* divine Beauty. The same *person* who grew and changed *in his human nature* remains immutable and timelessly eternal *in his divine nature*. He can reveal the Trinity's beauty to us precisely because that beauty is *his*. God the Son is infinite in virtue of his divine nature, and God the Son is finite in virtue of his human nature.

Sidebar 2.3
Extra Calvinisticum

The "*extra calvinisticum*" is a termed coined in the seventeenth century to describe the theological position of Christ's divine existence beyond his flesh. The term was coined originally as something of an insult. At that time, Lutheran and Reformed theologians were debating the nature of Christ's real presence in the Lord's Supper, and Lutherans referred to the Reformed teaching that Christ's omnipresence could not be communicated to his human nature and must therefore be attributed to his divine nature (see Sidebar 3.4). They accused the Reformed, in other words, of novelty—it was Calvin's doctrine of Christ's extra life. For their own part, the Reformed theologians insisted that their practice of distinguishing claims one can attribute to him in virtue of his divine nature from those one can attribute to him in virtue of his human nature was a way of maintaining the integral distinction of Christ's two natures—without abstracting them from the single divine person.

And lest you assume that my tone here is one of a typical theologian—stuck on a personal hobbyhorse and elevating the importance of an obscure doctrine past its proper height—we should recon with the fact that this doctrine is apparently important enough to be codified in *confessional form*. When the reformer Zacharias Ursinus penned the Heidelberg Catechism in 1563, we can be certain that he was not motivated by a fixation with tertiary topics. The purpose of a catechism like the Heidelberg Catechism is

to instruct young and new believers on the essentials of Christianity. Only the most important topics make the cut. When traditions and denominations adopt a catechism, like numerous traditions have done with the Heidelberg Catechism, they thereby make a statement about what they consider to be central and non-negotiable doctrines. So, when we come across questions 47 and 48 of the Heidelberg Catechism, we shouldn't dismiss them as unimportant idiosyncrasies. After affirming Christ's bodily ascension in question 46, the next two questions and answers read thus:

> *Question 47: But isn't Christ with us until the end of the world as he promised us?*
> **Answer:** Christ is true man and true God. In his human nature Christ is not now on earth; *but in his divinity, majesty, grace, and Spirit he is never absent from us.*

> *Question 48: If his humanity is not present wherever his divinity is, then aren't the two natures of Christ separated from each other?*
> **Answer:** Certainly not. Since divinity is not limited and is present everywhere, it is evident that *Christ's divinity is surely beyond the bounds of his humanity that has been taken on*, but at the same time his divinity is in and remains personally united to his humanity.[15]

The person of Christ is no less than his human nature. That human who lived and died and rose and ascended and will one day return *really is Christ,* the Second Person of the Trinity. He is human, yes, and he is infinitely more. His person is truly human in nature, but his person is not circumscribed by his human nature. Christ *exceeds.* Here is how I articulate this point in the form of a Sonnet entitled, Immanuel:

---

15. "The Heidelberg Catechism" in Van Dixhoorn, *Creeds*, p. 304.

O ever-generated Son of God
Motherless, beginningless, begotten
Late in time, born to walk the ground we've trod
Fatherless Son of the humble maiden
By Your Father are You true Light of Light
By Your mother are You true Man for us
Yet One You are, now come at our midnight
God and Man: depth of the mysterious
Come and transfigure my weak intellect
Bring my mind past the veil of unknowing
Bind what's broken to that which is perfect
Reconcile earth's song to heaven's ringing
Let me gaze upon You with the soul's eyes
May Your beauty assuage her every sigh.

All this is why you should feel absolutely no embarrassment or shame in reading through the gospels while worshiping *Jesus Christ*, the man—son of Mary, brother to James, cousin to John, eater of fish, drinker of wine. The man who *said* things and *felt* things and *did* things with his hands. You should feel absolutely no embarrassment about longing to hug his resurrected body with your resurrected body—and feel no embarrassment about longing for the day when you can look into his *human* eyes and say "thank you," and to watch his *human* lips curl into a *human* smile. In case you've forgotten, the incarnation is an ongoing reality. The Second person of the Trinity is and will forever be the God-*man*, Jesus Christ, because we will always and forever need that kind of accommodation! In the incarnation, God provides for our needs with the most beautiful man to ever exist.

* * *

O Triune God—you who are the fount of all beauty, you who inhabits your own eternity, which is marked by blessedness inexpressible—we thank you for the incarnation. Father of

lights, thank you for sending your Light in the flesh. Revealing Spirit, thank you for illumining our vision to behold Beauty enfleshed. Dear Jesus, thank you for revealing your glory—the glory of the infinite Trinity—to our unworthy eyes. Quicken the eyes of our minds and hearts to apprehend with gratitude and wonder the eternal loveliness revealed in the incarnation. For you, Jesus, have accommodated heaven for earthlings like us. In the incarnation, you have made invisible glory visible. Grant us the privilege of beholding your beauty in the pages of your holy Word. In your lovely name, Lord Jesus, Amen

3

The Hypostatic Union

You Might (Accidentally!) Believe in a Heresy

"I just keep failing. I know I'm a failure and I just walk around being reminded of how much of a failure I am." I sat across the table from a distraught church member, trying to process his words. His love of Christ had grown cold and his motivation for cultivating just about every relationship in his life—including his relationship with his wife—was gone. Things were getting bad, and as his pastor, I sought to intervene. "Sometimes I don't even want to get better," he went on, "I'm just so tired. My heart is cold and numb. And honestly, I don't even want to be here talking to you right now. I don't think there's anything you can say to me right now to make me care." There you have it. That was the situation. Although my body was frozen in my chair, I frantically scrambled for a response. Clearly, this brother was depressed by his persistent sin and calluses had encrusted over his soul. What was I to say?

A potential response could have been something like, "Hey brother, nobody's perfect. Hang in there and don't be so down on yourself for 'failing.' We're all failures from time to time, right? Just look on the bright side. Tomorrow is a

new day!" But I couldn't offer that response. There are *many* reasons why I couldn't say anything like this, the principle reason being that such a response is predicated on a lie. It's not true that "nobody's perfect." It's also not true that "we're *all* failures from time to time."

I have met one perfect man.

He is earnest and consistent through and through. He has never spoken an ill-timed word. I have seen him interact with the grieving, the arrogant, the indignant, the terrified, the apathetic, and the desperate, and every word in every occasion fit every need with surgeon-like precision. Even though some interactions have been difficult to watch, and his words have been jarring and offensive, upon deep reflection, I've never been able to pin a wrong on him.

I've seen him roar at evil like a lion and lounge with children on a hillside like a lamb.

He has frightened me with anger, comforted me with his kindness, and emboldened me with his leadership.

I have seen him showcase the perfection of humanity: elegance and grace and compassion, deep and dynamic like the ocean; and conviction and power and strength, firm and resolute like steel.

I have heard him pray perfect prayers, utter indignant words with perfect anger, weep perfectly sad tears, encourage with perfect affection, correct with perfect chastisement, offend with perfect integrity, beg God with perfect fervency, and deny himself with perfect love. And this is a *man* I am talking about—a true human being. One of us.

I am, of course, talking about the most beautiful man to ever live: Jesus Christ.

So, you see, I could not offer the false comfort to my church member that his failures were alright based on the inaccurate premise that all people are failures. Not all

people *are* failures. My friend's failures were not, therefore, acceptable defacto. While the perfection of Jesus might seem irrelevant to this situation, let me assure you, it is not. *Of course Jesus was perfect*, we are tempted to think, *he was the God-man. That isn't the point here. Jesus doesn't count.* But as we will see, Jesus's perfection does indeed count where it most matters, and that is precisely the point. It is the glorious, heart-stopping point of this chapter.

A Deficient Gospel

Christ's perfect life doesn't often get a lot of attention in our gospel presentations. We typically gloss over those thirty years (give or take) with "and he lived the perfect life that you and I could never live," before we get to the *really important* stuff about his death. Now, to be fair, these proportions seem to fit the mold of the New Testament Gospels themselves. After all, Matthew and Luke are the only two gospels who offer any details surrounding Christ's birth, and Luke is the only one who connects the dots between Jesus's boyhood and his public ministry—a feat he accomplishes with one swift sentence: "And Jesus increased in wisdom and in stature and in favor with God and man" (Luke 2:52). Additionally, the cross seems to be the gospel's most prominent theme throughout the rest of the New Testament. Paul once declared that he had decided "to know nothing among [the Corinthians] except Christ and him crucified" (1 Cor. 2:1). Paul was a man who truly believed that a simple gospel centered on the cross was the power of God for salvation (Rom. 1:16)

Evangelicals love preaching about the bloody cross. And they *should*! Without a bloody cross there is no gospel. Far be it for me to suggest we should ever preach a less bloody gospel. Nevertheless, we should not confuse simplicity for

reductionism. If we aren't careful, we can walk away with the impression that the sinner's only need—and Christ's only provision—is forgiveness. Of course, the good news of the gospel contains nothing *less* than the forgiveness of sins. But I'm going to argue here in this chapter that it contains *far more*. I am fond of reminding folks, that Paul's statement to the Corinthians about safeguarding a distinct gospel-simplicity does not amount to his saying, "I determined to know nothing among you except the *crucifixion*." He determined, rather, to know *Christ,* and *him* crucified. Who exactly is this Christ, and what is it that makes his crucifixion so important?

What is the Hypostatic Union?

When we ask the question, "Who is the Christ?" we are immediately thrust into a complex discussion of the identity of Israel's God and complicated-sounding terms like *hypostatic union.* If we aren't careful, those of us who have been steeped in Christian circles can lose the dizzying sense of wonder that these questions rightly elicit. These are not ordinary ideas, they are *weird* and *wonderful.*

In his helpful book, *Trinitarian Dogmatics,* D. Glenn Butner reminds us, "If we are to develop a dogmatic account of the divine missions," which includes events like the incarnation and the Spirit's work on Pentecost, "we must begin from a position of surprise, returning to the scandal and stumbling block of the salvific work of God (1 Cor. 1:23; 1 Pet. 2:8)."[1] For those of us who live in a world where Christianity has existed for two millennia, it can be easy for us to take doctrines like the Trinity and Christ's incarnation

---

1. D. Glenn Butner, *Trinitarian Dogmatics: Exploring the Grammar of the Christian Doctrine of God* (Grand Rapids, MI: Baker Academic, 2022), p. 168.

for granted. Even if we are new to the faith, and once thought the idea of the Trinity was crazy, most of us will have at least had some notion of people called "Christians" who believed in this idea. Few are shocked to hear of a group of people who claim to be monotheists, but whose one God is somehow also three, Father, Son, and Spirit.

But it is helpful for us to remind ourselves of how this idea must have landed on people in Jesus's day. At that time in the Greco-Roman world, there were monotheists and there were polytheists—those who believed in one mono-personal God, and those who believed in many gods—and that was it. Those were pretty much your only two options in first century Rome. So, for God to reveal progressively over time that this one God exists eternally as *Father, Son, and Spirit*—a tri-personal God—was a massive paradigm shift.

In contrast to the tribal deities of the surrounding pagan nations, or the pantheon of gods accepted in the Greco-Roman world, Israel was to worship *one* God who created heaven and earth: "Hear, O Israel: the LORD our God, the LORD is one" (Deut. 6:4). With the advent of Christ, and within the flow of God's continual self-revelation, something marvelous begins to happen. The prophetic witness of Christ and his apostles begin to describe three distinct persons with divine language, attributing divine descriptions not just to the *Father,* but also to the Son, and the Spirit. And yet, at no point in the New Testament do we see Christ or the apostles back away from the former Old Testament claims regarding *monotheism.* They are not, in their own self-conception, theological revisionists. They do not add an asterisk to their monotheistic claims. Instead, Christ and his apostles uniformly *double down* on the claim that there is one and only one God, even when they make breathtaking

statements about three distinct persons (John 17:3; Rom. 3:30; 1 Tim. 1:17; James 2:19).

In fact, that anthem we just read from Deuteronomy 6:4 is picked up in New Testament revelation and is *Christianized*. Paul quotes this verse but puts Christ into it in 1 Corinthians 8:6: "yet for us there is one God, the Father, from whom are all things and for whom we exist, and one Lord, Jesus Christ, through whom are all things and through whom we exist." All things exist *from* and *for* the Father, and *through* the Son. And this is no rogue imposition on Paul's part, as if he is putting words in Jesus's mouth. Jesus himself takes the name of Israel's covenant-making, covenant-keeping God as *his own*, when he says, "before Abraham was, *I am*." (John 8:58).

No Jewish follower of Jesus in his day or thereafter was asked to abandon his former embrace of monotheism. In fact, every Jewish Christian was explicitly *forbade* to do this. To be a Christian is to follow the monotheistic ways of the Old Testament. The Jews were to worship Yahweh—and Christ is Yahweh enfleshed. The Athanasian Creed has good and biblical warrant for insisting that "just as Christian truth compels us to confess each person [Father, Son, and Spirit] as both God and Lord, so catholic religion forbids us to say that there are three gods or lords."[2] Unless we are completely oblivious to the gravity of the Bible's portrayal of God as *one* and of Christ as God the Son incarnate, the only fitting way for us to approach Christology is in a state of perpetual and delighted *surprise*.

Remaining in this state of delighted surprise is a helpful safeguard to preserve our praise. If we maintain this disposition, we will find ourselves eager to plumb the depth of meaning behind the central confession that Jesus Christ

---

2. "The Athanasius Creed" in Van Dixhoorn, *Creeds*, pp. 21-22.

is *God the Son incarnate* with fitting language. Jesus is he who is God and who, without ceasing to be God, became man "for us and for our salvation." He, the one who saved us and the one whom we love, is one person in two natures. In the face of these staggering claims, we should be asking, *How should we praise him? What is the right language to use? How can I describe him in a way that doesn't explain away the mystery, but rather preserves the mystery for proper praise? I don't want to say anything unbecoming of him! What are the right categories to think with?*

Sidebar 3.1
Hypostatic Union

The hypostatic union refers to the union that exists between Christ's two natures. *Hypostasis* refers to the single person—the Son—and *union* refers to the Son's union to either nature. The hypostatic union affirms that the single person of Christ is united to two distinct natures that remain unconfused and unmixed, but nevertheless united to one and only one subject—one "who;" one person, the Son. All that it means to be divine, the Son is, and all that it means to be human, the Son is.

As we ask those questions—the questions that bubble up from the disposition of delighted surprise—we can gratefully receive answers from the Great Tradition of the Christian faith. Of course, we ought not slavishly adhere to the Great Tradition in a mindless way. Rather, since we are eager to praise Christ with language that befits him, we humbly and gratefully acknowledge the inheritance of our family tree. Our forefathers in the faith have thought on these matters diligently, and they have given us words and categories we might otherwise find intimidating or needlessly obscure (like the hypostatic union), but in this state of delighted surprise,

we will gladly take anything that helps us to more adequately praise the one by whom we are continually surprised.

Along these lines, we can thank God for the Chalcedonian Statement on Christology, which summarizes the union of Christ's two natures with *extra-biblical language* that serves to *uphold biblical teaching*, over and against the heresies of its day, which used *biblical language* in order to *undermine biblical teaching*. These heresies included (but were not limited to) Nestorianism (which stressed the distinction of Christ's natures to the neglect of their union in the single Person, sometimes implying that the divine Son and the human Christ were two separate personalities—two distinct entities) and Apollinarianism (which denied that the Son assumed a human soul, and rather only assumed a human body animated by a divine will). Against both extremes, the Church Fathers who gathered at Chalcedon threaded the orthodox needle to articulate biblical truth with razor-sharp precision. Here is their statement in full:

> Following the saintly fathers, we all with one voice teach the confession of one and the same Son, our Lord Jesus Christ: the same perfect in divinity and perfect in humanity, the same truly God and truly man, of a rational soul and a body; consubstantial with the Father as regards his divinity, and the same consubstantial with us as regards his humanity; like us in all respects except for sin; begotten before the ages from the Father as regards his divinity, and in the last days the same for us and for our salvation from Mary, the virgin God-bearer, as regards his humanity; one and the same Christ, Son, Lord, only-begotten, acknowledged in two natures which undergo no confusion, no change, no division, no separation; at no point was the difference between the natures taken away through the union, but rather the property of both natures is preserved and comes together into a single person and a single subsistent being;

he is not parted or divided into two persons, but is one and the same only-begotten Son, God, Word, Lord Jesus Christ, just as the prophets taught from the beginning about him, and as the Lord Jesus Christ himself instructed us, and as the creed of the fathers handed it down to us.[3]

Sidebar 3.2
Chalcedon Definition

The Chalcedon Definition is a theological position statement on the person of Christ produced in the fifth century during the council at Chalcedon, which was held in 451. This council, known as the fourth ecumenical council, was convened in order to resolve a series of Christological controversies, which arose chiefly from Nestorius of Constantinople (A.D. 386–451) and Cyril of Alexandria (d. A.D. 444). Nestorius's teaching— which seemed to imply so sharp a distinction between Christ's two natures (divine and human) so as to imply a separation of two persons— was condemned at the council, and the "Definition" was produced as something of a Christological appendix to the Nicene Creed, in order to interpret how Christ's two natures relate to one another in the one person.

Notice, first of all, the language which affirm the Son's *divine* nature ("same perfect in Godhead..." "truly God..." "consubstantial with the Father according to the Godhead..." "begotten before all ages of the Father according to the Godhead..."). These statements affirm not only the equality of the Son with the Father, but they also describe how the Son relates eternally to the Father. He is "begotten before all ages of the Father according to the Godhead." What distinguishes the Son from the Father in eternity is that the Son *comes from* the Father. This description of the Father as the "Source" of the Son, shouldn't lead us to believe that the Son is in any way subordinate or less than the Father—he is,

---

3. "The Chalcedonian Definition," in Van Dixhoorn, *Creeds*, p. 27.

after all, *consubstantial* with the Father. And this is because the divine nature is not separate from the divine persons. It's not as if there is an abstract category (God) and three persons who each fit within it (Father, Son, and Spirit). The divine nature *is eternally* Father, Son, and Spirit. The Father never *started* generating the Son; the eternal Father eternally generates the Son. That's what it means for the Father to be Father—he is eternally Father *of the* Son, and the Son, likewise, is eternally Son *of the* Father.

Notice, secondly, the affirmation of Jesus's *human* nature ("perfect in manhood…" "truly man, of a rational soul and body…" "consubstantial with us according to the manhood; in all things like unto us, without sin…" "in these latter days, for us and for our salvation, born of the Virgin Mary… according to the manhood…"). These statements affirm that the Son, in the womb of Mary, took on a nature that was without sin, and was yet truly and completely human. As he is eternally "coessential with the Father according to the Godhead," he became "coessential with us according to the manhood." This means that whatever it means to be truly human, Jesus was that. This is why we see that line, "of a rational soul and body." All the things that come with being a human (consciousness, will, desire, memory, soul, body) Jesus assumed.

Thus far, our observations show that the Fathers at Chalcedon firmly rejected Apollinarianism. But many of these statements regarding the divine nature of the Son and the human natures of Christ could be affirmed by a Nestorian as well. This is why the Chalcedonian statement *also* contains descriptions that emphasize the mystery of these two natures uniting in the *single* person of the Son. These two natures don't blend with one another, nor do they split Christ up into two persons (one divine and one human). The one whom we

consider in this statement is "the same Son, our Lord Jesus Christ … one and the same Christ, Son, Lord, Only-begotten, to be acknowledged in two natures, without confusion, without change, without division, without separation … the distinction of natures being by no means taken away by the union … the property of each nature being preserved, and concurring in one person and one subsistence, not parted or divided into two persons, but one and the same Son, and only begotten, God the Word, the Lord Jesus Christ…" Thus, the Fathers at Chalcedon rejected Nestorianism as well. If this were not clear from the statements above, it is made explicit from the description of Mary as "the God-bearer," or "the Mother of God," which was repugnant to the Nestorians, and probably rubs not a few evangelicals today the wrong way. Which, I think, calls for a bit further explanation.

Should Evangelicals Call Mary the "Mother of God"?

The question of what to do with Mary the mother of Jesus is not one evangelicals consider very often. It is easy to simply dismiss the notion that *any* careful consideration of Mary should be made. Isn't honoring Mary a Roman Catholic thing? This general ethos can cause evangelicals to get particularly squeamish around the language of *theotokos* (the God-bearer, or the Mother of God) in the Chalcedonian Statement on Christology. There is good reason, however, for maintaining the language in the Statement, but to get a clear picture, we should go all the way back to the beginning.

In the garden of Eden, after Adam had disobeyed God and before he was forced out of the garden, God promised in Genesis 3:15 that a seed would come from the *woman*, who would crush the head of the Serpent, thereby turning back the curse and putting an end to the enmity between man and God. This Seed, therefore, would need to be a *new Adam*—a new

head of a new human race, since the first head of the first human race had fallen. This, in part, is why the seed would come from *woman*, even though "seed" naturally comes from man. All men, and heads of all households, are *fallen in Adam*. Therefore, for a new human race to begin, a new head would have to be provided—one that had not received the sin-pollution of the first head. Paul tells us plainly that this Seed—this Second Adam—is Christ—in Romans 5:12-21, and 1 Corinthians 15:20-28.

Mary, therefore, is "the" woman promised in Genesis 3:15.

Sidebar 3.3
Nestorianism

Nestorianism gets its name from Nestorius of Constantinople (A.D. 386–451), a presbyter who clashed with Cyril of Alexandria (d. 446) in the fifth century over Christology. Nestorius is known for objecting to the title given to Mary that would eventually be codified in the Chalcedonian Definition, *theotokos* (God-bearer), on account of his belief that this confused the divine and human natures of Christ. According to his opponents, however, Nestorius's teaching distinguished between the divine and human natures of Christ so sharply that they seemed to imply a distinction not only of natures (divine and human), but also of *persons* (the Logos and Jesus Christ). Nestorius was condemned in the third, fourth, and fifth ecumenical councils (the Council of Ephesus in 431, the Council of Chalcedon in 451 [see Sidebar 3.2], and the Second Council of Constantinople in 553).

Just think about the honor thereby bestowed on her: in God's providence, she is used to fulfill the oldest divine prophecy ever uttered. Her son is the promised Seed. *All of Christ's humanity comes from Mary.* It is the flesh that *she gave him* that redeems the universe. The body that grew in *her womb* would grow to become the body of the Second Adam of a new humanity that *she would become a part of.* It is the flesh that grew in her that would become her own salvation. It is

the flesh that grew in her womb that would become the head of a new family—the Christian family.

Evangelicals rightly feel a deep aversion to the Mariology of the Roman Catholic Church, whose unbiblical teaching on Mary is, we would say, positively *idolatrous*. She is no co-*mediatrix* (co-mediator with Christ). Christians do not need her to intercede before Christ, for Christ to intercede before the Father, since there is one mediator between God and man, the man Christ Jesus (1 Tim. 2:5). She must not receive prayer for *any* reason. She was a sinner, saved by grace through faith *in her Son*. She was a disciple of Jesus along with the rest of the disciples. She enjoyed the grace of marriage and marital intimacy with Joseph and bore other sons. She died and was buried like every other descendent of Adam, and her body awaits resurrection and reunion with her soul, which is in the presence of Christ—her Son and her Savior—like every other Christian.

And yet, she was blessed in a truly unique way! The Chalcedonian statement on Christology calls Mary the "mother of God" for good reason. Not only does it have biblical warrant (Elizabeth, after all, called the pregnant Mary "mother of my Lord"), it also shores up an important theological truth.

On the one hand, what grew inside Mary's womb was a *human being*—a real person of a human body and soul. The Spirit supernaturally fertilized her egg to form within her womb a *true human*—not a superhuman or a demigod. The "what" of that little person in her womb is "human." And yet, on the other hand, the identity of that human nature—the "who" of the embryonic human nature from conception—was *God the Son*. This is what the designation "mother of God" safeguards. *Theotokos* is more of a statement on Christ than it is a statement on Mary. So, while this term has been

abused by the Roman Catholic Church, this doesn't mean that the term—or the biblical truth it articulates—should be minimized or rejected. Mary is the mother of God the Son. She is the mother not of his *divine* nature, but rather only his *human* nature. And yet it is *he*—God the Son—whom she mothered. The Son is begotten from the Father *before all time*, and begotten of Mary, the mother of God, born *in time*.

Recall that doctrine we examined in the previous chapter: the *communication of idioms*. Because the Son of God is coessential with the Father in his divine nature and coessential with us according to his human nature, whatever can be predicated of either nature (divine or human) can be said of the Son, but this does not mean that whatever can be said of either nature can be said of *the other nature*.

Is the Son timelessly eternal in his life—with no beginning and no end? *Yes*, according to the Godhead.

Did the Son grow from infanthood and die on the cross? *Yes*, according to manhood.

Is the Son unchangeable—or *immutable*? *Yes*, according to the Godhead.

Did the Son change and grow and get hungry and tired? *Yes*, according to manhood.

Is the Son omniscient—all knowing? *Yes*, according to the Godhead.

Was the Son ignorant of certain things in the gospel? *Yes*, according to manhood.

Does the Son have all divine authority? *Yes*, according to the Godhead.

Does the Son obey and submit to the Father's higher authority? *Yes*, according to manhood.

We can say all these things about Christ. Jesus is immutable (unchangeable) and *mutable* (changeable). He is *changeless* in virtue of his divine nature, and he *changes* in virtue of his human nature. And because these natures are united to the *person of Christ*, and not to *the divine nature itself*, the divine nature remains perfect in the incarnation. In other words, we cannot say that the divine nature, as such, grew tired or suffered or died. Rather, the divine Son, on account of his *human* nature, grew tired and suffered and died.

Sidebar 3.4
Communicatio Idiomatum

Communicatio idiomatum, or the communication of idioms (or properties) is a term shared by many Christian traditions, though signifies different teachings depending on the tradition. The Lutheran teaching of the *communicatio idiomatum* teaches that idioms or properties of Christ's two natures can be communicated to one another on account of the hypostatic union, such that Christ's human nature—which would not otherwise be possibly present in communion meals celebrated across time and space, for example, since human nature is not omnipresent—is truly present at the Lord's Table since the divine attribute of omnipresence is *communicated* to Christ via the hypostatic union. The *communicatio idiomatum* for Lutheranism, then, means that certain attributes from one nature can be communicated to another on account of the hypostatic union. For the Calvinist tradition, however, the *communicatio idiomatum* is a way of *distinguishing* between properties that can be attributed to Christ according to either nature. Anything that can be essentially affirmed of divinity and anything that can be essentially affirmed of humanity can be essentially affirmed of Christ, but that does not mean that anything that can be essentially affirmed of *divinity* can be essentially affirmed of humanity and vise versa. E.g., Christ is immutable (unchangeable) because of his divine nature, and he is mutable (changeable) by virtue of his human nature, but that does not mean that the divine nature is changeable or that human nature is unchangeable.

Reading Christ Rightly in the Scriptures

Once we grasp this, we are helped tremendously in the way we read the Scriptures. If this is, in fact, how the Scriptures present Christ to us, then it seems they commend what we call *partitive exegesis.*[4] Partitive exegesis is born out of the conviction that *everything* the Bible says about Jesus is true. This way of reading the Bible is a way of affirming all that Scripture says about Jesus without making Scripture contradict itself. It asks the question, "Is this *true statement* about Jesus true on account of his divine nature, or is it true on account of his human nature?"

Sidebar 3.5
Exegesis / Partitive Exegesis

Exegesis is a term that describes the work of interpreting the meaning of a text. To exegete is to *draw out* the meaning of a given text. *Partitive* Exegesis names particular strategy to interpret passages about the person and nature of Christ. Partitive Exegesis presupposes the unity—without confusion or separation—of Christ's two natures and seeks to determine how any given description of Christ in Holy Scripture relates to those natures. In other words, Partitive Exegesis, which affirms that all Scripture says of Christ is true, provides the interpreter with tools to attribute certain descriptions of Christ to him by virtue of his *human* nature (e.g. descriptions that include him growing, changing, dying, etc.), and others by virtue of his *divine* nature (e.g. descriptions of his authority to raise and judge the dead, forgive sins, have life in himself, etc.), while maintaining the unity of his person.

So, for example, in the Scriptures, we learn that Jesus dies (Matt. 27:50). This is true of the one person, Christ. But is it true on account of his divine nature? Well, the divine nature

---

4. For more on partitive exegesis, see R.B. Jamieson and Tyler R. Wittman, *Biblical Reasoning: Christological and Trinitarian Rules for Exegesis* (Grand Rapids, MI: Baker Academic, 2022).

can't die. So we know that it must be true of him on account of his human nature. Additionally, in the Scriptures, Jesus says he will be with us to the end of the age (Matt. 28:20). This is true of the one person, Jesus Christ. But is it true on account of his human nature? Well, human nature isn't *omnipresent*—human nature cannot be *everywhere*. So, this must be true of Christ on account of his divine nature.

Here's the point of partitive *exegesis*: When we see Jesus doing things that only God has divine authority to do, he is doing them by virtue of his divine nature (forgiving sins, receiving worship, authoritatively commanding nature, etc.). On the other hand, when we see Jesus doing things that only creatures can do, he is doing them by virtue of his human nature (growing tired, changing, dying, obeying, etc.).

Why does all of this matter so much for us? Why should we labor to stress the importance of the union (without confusion, division, or separation) of Christ's human nature and divine nature? Why should we labor to stress what Christ does *as man*, and what Christ does *as God*? It matters because these truths also have deep consequences on the work of Christ on our behalf.

You Might Believe in a Heresy

Actually, you might believe in *two* heresies. Do not be alarmed! It's an accident, I'm sure. Most of us assume these heresies when we describe the union of Christ's two natures, but it's up to us to scrub our imaginations and speech of these heresies. The first one I've mentioned already: Apollinarianism. You might have been a bit confused a moment ago when I mentioned that in the incarnation, Christ assumed a *human soul*. What does that mean exactly? It means that the incarnation was *not* the moment when the divine Son took on a human *body*, which was animated by a

divine soul. This kind of "incarnation" is what Apollinarians believed and it is unorthodox. And yet, most Christians, if they had to describe the incarnation and the relationship between Christ's two natures, would sound remarkably Apollinarian. Trevin Wax describes his own experience as an accidental adherent to heresy in this way:

> I used to believe a heresy. Not intentionally, of course. I discovered my error during my first year of theology classes in Romania. Our systematic theology professor listed heresies of the Trinitarian variety and arrived at Apollinarianism, which he described as "the teaching that Jesus had a divine soul in a human body." I felt like someone had punched me in the gut. Though this heresy had never been taught in my church, it had somehow wormed its way into my mind as the most logical way to hold Christ's divinity and humanity together. I'd just assumed that Jesus as "God in the flesh" meant a divine mind/spirit wrapped up in a human body.
>
> Logical or not, it was wrong. I was wrong. This doesn't mean I wasn't a true believer in Christ. I had been seeking for years to faithfully follow Jesus, which is why I wound up studying theology in Romania in the first place. My understanding of Christ's nature was in error, but I was a genuine believer. Once my error was contradicted by the testimony of Scripture and witness of the church through the ages, I corrected my understanding and never looked back.[5]

So, if you—like Wax and many more—have been an accidental Apollinarian, don't worry: this doesn't mean you aren't a Christian. It does mean, however, that I have just made things difficult for you. By letting you know you've been an unwitting heretic, I've ruined your happy ignorance

---

5. Trevin Wax, *The Thrill of Orthodoxy: Rediscovering the Adventure of Christian Faith* (Downers Grove, IL: IVP, 2022), p. 50.

and have placed a wonderful burden on you. No longer do you have the luxury of not investigating this question: why is Apollinarianism a heresy? The stakes are now too high for you to ignore that question. You *have to* answer it now. What I'm about to say is therefore incredibly important, so buckle up.

The short answer to our question is that the Apollinarian incarnation is an incarnation of less than true humanity. Humans, by nature, are composites of body and soul. If Christ only assumed a body, but not a human soul, he didn't assume a whole human nature. He isn't truly human. So, the short answer to the question, "why is Apollinarianism a heresy?" is: Apollinarianism doesn't truly affirm the incarnation of Christ. A longer answer to the question involves our consideration of another related heresy you might inadvertently believe: *monothelitism*.

The council that determined *monothelitism* as a heresy was Constantinople III (681), the third ecumenical council in the city of Constantinople, and the sixth ecumenical council of the early Church.[6] *Monothelites* insisted that the person of Christ had a single will (*mono* = one; *thelite* = will), while those who adhered to *dyothelitism* insisted that Christ had two wills (*dyo* = two; *thelite* = will)—one will for his human nature, and another for his divine. These two errors— Apollinarianism and *monothelitism*—are interrelated, for the *will* and the *soul* are intimately connected. The will is a faculty of the soul, so, to have a soul is to have a will (and *vice versa*).

This being the case, a human will is essential to a human nature, and so the stakes on the question of whether

---

6. It is worth mentioning that not all Protestants accept all seven of the seven ecumenical councils. Typically, the only council Protestants (rightly) object to is the seventh, Nicaea II (787), which rendered the veneration of icons and prayers to the saints compulsory, anathematizing dissenters.

Christ assumed a unique human *will* in the incarnation are therefore just as high as on the question of whether he assumed a human *soul*. Unless we affirm that Christ assumed a human *soul* with a human *will*, we are left with two disastrous conclusions—one that jeopardizes the Trinity, and the other that jeopardizes the incarnation (and therefore, our salvation).

Sidebar 3.6
Apollinarianism

Apollinarianism gets is name from Apollinaris of Laodicea (d. 382). Apollinaris was a disciple of the great Athanasius (d. 373) and strident critic of Arianism (see Sidebar 2.1). To Apollinaris, one of the most tragic consequences of Arianism is that it makes salvation impossible—man's restoration to God cannot, according to Apollinaris, be secured by the will or the soul of a corruptible creature. Therefore, in order to avoid this error of Arianism, Apollinaris went so far as to deny that Christ had a human soul or will *at all*; rather, in his teaching, the incarnation was the divine Son's assumption of a human flesh that remained animated by a divine soul and will. Unfortunately, this would mean that the Son's incarnation is not his assumption of a genuine human *nature*, since human nature is a composite of body and (human) soul. Apollinarianism was condemned in the second ecumenical council, Constantinople I (381).

Monothelitism / Dyothelitism

Monothelitism and Dyothelitism describe opposite positions of a Christological controversy that arose toward the end of the seventh century. Monothelites taught that Christ had *one* will (*mono* = one; *thelite* = will), while the Dyothelites taught that he had *two* wills to correspond with his two natures (*dyo* = two; *thelite* = will). The ecumenical council of the early church, Constantinople III, convened to resolve this controversy, and concluded that the Monothelitism compromised the integrity of the distinction (without confusion or separation) of Christ's two natures, and was therefore to be rejected as heresy.

On the one hand, if Christ did not assume a human soul with a human will in the incarnation, then we would have to conclude that the Trinity is a composition of three subjects with three wills (and, probably, three centers of consciousness). How so? Well, we would have to conclude from events like Christ's prayer in the garden of Gethsemane, when he says to the Father, "Not as I will, but as you will" (Matt. 26:39), that such an event is the divine will of the Son submitting to the divine will of the Father. If he has only one will, and that one will is his divine will, then the distinction between *his* will and the *Father's* ("not as I will, but as you will") cannot be the distinction between a human will and the divine will, but rather between two divine wills. But if our Trinity is a *composition* of three subjects with three wills, we are just a stone's throw away from tritheism, which is a particular kind of polytheism.

On the other hand, if Christ did not assume a human soul with a human will, then he did not assume a *human nature*. To put the matter plainly: humans don't have divine souls or divine wills. So, if you happen to come across a thing that looks like a young Jewish man—say, praying in a garden and sweating blood, for example—who has a human body but a *divine* soul and will, you have found something truly remarkable! But it isn't *human*.

If this kind of incarnation were the case—the assumption of a human body with a divine soul or spirit—the gospel would be utterly compromised. Why? Because, the perfect obedience of a divine will cannot be attributed to *human beings* who have human wills! Therefore, the merit of *righteousness* acquired by the *obedience* of such a will cannot be *imputed* to human beings. Our problem is a human problem, and as such, it needs a human solution.

Think back on that moment in the garden of Gethsemane. On whose account did Christ resolve to obey the divine will and go to the cross? If the *monothelites* are right, we sort of have to say that he did this on *his own* account. It is the will of a divine person bowing to the will of another divine person for the sake of divine harmony in the society of divine wills. But if the *dyothelites* are right (and they are), Christ did this on *our* account. Consider these words from Maximus the Confessor:

> It follows, then, that having become like us for our sake, he was calling on his God and Father in a human manner when he said, *Let not what I will, but what you will prevail,* inasmuch as, being God by nature, he also in his humanity has, as his human volition, the fulfillment of the will of the Father. This is why, considering both of the natures from which, in which, and of which his person was, he is acknowledged as able both to will and to effect our salvation. As God, he approved that salvation along with the Father and the Holy Spirit; as man, he *became* for the sake of salvation *obedient* to his Father *unto death, even death on a cross* (Phil. 2:8). He accomplished this great feat of the economy of salvation for our sake through the mystery of the incarnation.[7]

Christ submitted a *human* will to the divine will on behalf of *humans.* Why? Because it was a human will that broke the law of God and brought sin into the world. It was a human will that racked up the wages of sin. It was a human will that corrupted all subsequent human wills (but one). And therefore, only a human will could pay those wages and restore those corruptions. Is it not clear, then, that the

---

7. St. Maximus the Confessor, *On the Cosmic Mystery of Jesus Christ: Selected Writings from St Maximus the Confessor,* Paul M. Blowers and Robert Louis Wilken (eds., trans.) (Crestwood, NY: St. Vladimir's Seminary Press, 2003), p. 176.

Christ of Holy Scripture and the Church's Great Tradition is incomparably more beautiful than his heretical and heterodox rivals?

A Tale of Two Adams

So much Christological error could be avoided if we paid proper attention to those glorious words in the Nicene Creed: "for us men and for our salvation." Consider Romans 5:12-21. What we find in this passage is a *tale of two Adams*. It is a *tale of two federal heads*, who act on behalf of all those whom they represent. Each human on this planet has one of two federal representatives: we are all either the posterity of Adam, or the Second Adam, Christ. We are either in the family tree of Adam, or the family tree of Christ. We are all born into the former, and some are born again into the latter—but autonomous self-independence is not possible. We don't get to repudiate our covenantal head. We don't get to emancipate ourselves from our federal representative.

In Romans 5:12, Paul explains how sin entered into the world, and set up its dominion with its vice regent, death. "Therefore, just as sin came into the world through one man, and death through sin, and so death spread to all men because all sinned …" Sin and death are personified here as tyrannical oppressors, keeping the whole human race under their thumb. Is this imagery not fitting? Does this not perfectly correspond to our lived experience on this planet? How many of us are familiar with the feeling of sin's fingers wrapped around our throats? How many of us have experienced the death of a loved one? Does it not feel like something *deeply wrong* has taken place? That deep and abiding feeling that we get—the feeling that says, "Something's not right. Something's broken;" that feeling that insists on *objecting* to death—that feeling should not be

ignored or brushed aside or dismissed. We ought never say, "Death is a part of life." It's *not*. That discontented feeling is communicating a deep truth: sin and death are illegitimate tyrants. Death is an intruder. It doesn't belong here. And Romans 5:12 tells us how "he" got here.

When Adam disobeyed God's command and ate from the tree of the knowledge of good and evil, he welcomed sin into this world, and sin brought Death with him. The world has never been the same. Why? Why is it that sin came into the world "through *one* man"? The answer is difficult to stomach for a world that prizes individuality and autonomy. The answer is that Adam acted on behalf of the entire human race. What we are talking about here is the crucial concept known as *federal headship*. God created Adam as the representative of his image bearers—he was to be humanity's covenant representative. The command God issued to him—to refrain from eating from the tree of good and evil—was a command he would obey or disobey *on behalf of everyone he represented*. When Adam disobeyed, his disobedience was imputed and attributed to all those under his headship, which was *the entire human race*. This is why the fall of mankind and the mark of original sin is laid at the feet of Adam and not Eve, even though Eve's disobedience preceded Adam's. Eve wasn't set up as the federal head of humanity, Adam was.

In addition to the legal guilt imputed to us, Adam also handed down a sin nature. "Death spread to all men because all sinned," and all sinned in Adam, not only legally, but also throughout time in history. Adam led humanity into the enslavement of sin and death. *That* is how this world came to taste death's bitter sting.

All this feels unfair to a world that obsesses over individuality and self-expression. Most of us are not primed

by our cultures to accept this notion. But we should accept it nonetheless, because it's biblical. Even a cursory glance at the Scripture demonstrates this. In the book of Numbers, for example, the nation of Israel plummets into idolatrous Baal worship at Peor, and God sent a plague that rapidly killed many in the nation (Num. 25:1-9). In response, Phinehas the priest executed two of the most brazen idolaters, and his one zealous act of faithfulness saved the nation from further spread of the plague (Num. 25:10-18). Phinehas acted on behalf of the whole nation—his righteous deed was accounted to the whole assembly. By contrast, toward the end of 2 Samuel, David sinfully and boastfully called for a census of the nation for no other reason than to gloat in his accomplishments, and as a result, God sent a pestilence and 70,000 men died (2 Sam. 24:1-17). David acted on behalf of the whole nation, and his unrighteous deed was accounted to everyone under his headship.

But not only is this notion of headship basic to the story of Scripture, it's basic to the world we live in. In recent years, a common catchphrase designed to vocalize political dissent has arisen in the United States of America: "Not my president." In many ways, this slogan perfectly encapsulates self-expressive individualism. It is the declaration of autonomous independence. *I don't identify myself with his presidency, therefore, he is not my president.* But this is an embarrassing delusion. One can say, "Not my president," all one wants, but when the president communicates with world leaders, who does he represent if not *the whole nation—* including those of us who say, "not my president?" For good or for ill, whoever is in the office represents the nation, and this principle applies in every direction: fathers represent their families, CEOs represent their companies, managers represent their stores, team captains represent their

teams, etc. On some level, this concept of representation is irreducibly part of this world. And we trace this all the way back to the schema of creation itself. It's God's design: the same design that renders Adam our federal head.

As we continue reading in Romans 5, we receive an answer to another question we may be asking: why was Adam representing humanity in that one sin, and not every sin he ever committed? Answer, because that one sin was an act of breaking covenant with God, and he was acting as our covenant representative. "For sin indeed was in the world before the law was given, but sin is not counted where there is no law. Yet death reigned from Adam to Moses, even over those whose sinning was not like the transgression of Adam, who was a type of the one who was to come" (Rom. 5:13-14) This passage deals with what Reformed theologians call *the Covenant of Works*—the covenant God entered into with mankind through the covenant representative, Adam, upon creation. The Covenant of Works had a couple of positive commands ("be fruitful and multiply and fill the earth and subdue the earth"), and it had *one* prohibition ("do not eat from the tree in the midst of the garden"). Perfect and complete obedience held out promise for eternal life, and disobedience guaranteed death. So, when Adam disobeyed, *he broke God's covenantal law.*

When Paul says, "sin was indeed in the world before the *law* was given," he refers to the Mosaic Law given at Sinai. But then he goes on to say, "sin is not counted where there is no law. Yet death reigned from Adam to Moses." So, there is no such thing as sin if there is no such thing as the law, since sin is a transgression of law. And there is no death without sin, since death is the penalty of sin. Yet we know sin existed before the Mosaic Law was given, because *death reigned* throughout that whole period of time ("from Adam

to Moses"). What does that mean? It means that there was a "law" before the "law was given"—there was a *law* that predated the Mosaic Law given at Sinai. If this were not the case, the presence of death from Adam to Moses would make no sense.

So, what is this law that Adam broke before the (Mosaic) law was given? It was God's moral law, which he gave to all humanity, beginning with Adam. This is the law that we are all bound to by virtue of being made in God's image. It's the law that all humanity breaks, as Paul says in Romans 1:18-24. That law was broken by our covenant representative, Adam—the head of humanity—and it is subsequently broken by everyone who came after him. And yet, on a hopeful note, Paul says that Adam "was a type of the one who was to come."

> But the free gift is not like the trespass. For if many died through one man's trespass, much more have the grace of God and the free gift by the grace of that one man Jesus Christ abounded for many. And the free gift is not like the result of that one man's sin. For the judgment following one trespass brought condemnation, but the free gift following many trespasses brought justification. For if, because of one man's trespass, death reigned through that one man, much more will those who receive the abundance of grace and the free gift of righteousness reign in life through the one man Jesus Christ.

> Therefore, as one trespass led to condemnation for all men, so one act of righteousness leads to justification and life for all men. For as by one man's disobedience the many were made sinners, so by the one man's obedience the many will be made righteous (Rom 5:15-19).

We may not like what Adam does on our behalf, but the same mechanism (i.e., federal headship) that renders his actions as counting for us also renders Christ's actions as counting

for us. Without the imputation of Adam's guilt, there is no imputation of the Second Adam's righteousness. There is a parallel between the works of Adam—the federal head of humanity—being imputed to *his* posterity, and the works of Jesus—the federal head of a new humanity—being imputed to his posterity. Adam stands in for all of humanity when he transgresses God, and his transgression is imputed to all those whom he represents. Likewise, Christ stands in for all his new humanity when he obeys God, and his righteousness is imputed to all those he represents.

"That Which He Has Not Assumed, He Has Not Healed"

Intrinsic in all of this is the concept of recapitulation. Christ is not merely offering a parallel alternative to Adam as another option. Rather, Christ is recapitulating humanity as it was intended. Adam's failure was a failure to obey and to thereby achieve the righteousness leading to eternal life. Therefore, when Jesus arrives as the sinless one, he is succeeding precisely where Adam failed. Calvin sums up this point nicely,

> Accordingly, our Lord came forth as true man and took the person and the name of Adam in order to take Adam's place in obeying the Father, to present our flesh as the price of satisfaction to God's righteous judgment, and, in the same flesh, to pay the penalty that we had deserved.[8]

This calls attention to a noteworthy question from our passage. What is Jesus's "obedience" here? We know what Adam's one transgression is (i.e., the act of taking the prohibited fruit). But what about Christ? What is *his* "one act of righteousness leading to justification?" What is his

---

8. Calvin, *Institutes*, 2.13.3.

"obedience" which makes many "righteous?" Well, narrowly considered, it is clear that Paul *at least* has the atoning death of Christ in view. After all, the culmination of Jesus's entire lifelong obedience hinges on that moment in the garden of Gethsemane, when his prayer concluded with "Not my will but yours be done." That was when the final decision for obedience was sealed to go to the cross, and at the cross of Christ, all these justifying benefits come to be filtered down to one point. The center of all human history is right here, at the cross of Christ. This is where atonement is made for sin, divine wrath is propitiated, the gift of the Spirit's indwelling presence is purchased with blood. The cross of Christ is the one crucial point in redemptive history where Christ is lifted up, and thereafter *draws all people to himself.* All the promises of God have been marching throughout human history to this point: the cross. They're all wrapped up *there*, on calvary, so they could be buried in his tomb, and subsequently spring forth in his resurrection.

But our understanding of Christ's "obedience" here cannot be *exhausted* by his atoning work on the cross. It must include more. We need, what Reformed theologians call, the *passive* and *active* obedience of Christ. Christ's *passive* obedience refers to his life of suffering—culminating with his death on the cross—whereby he bears the consequences of law-breaking. "By sending his own Son in the likeness of sinful flesh and for sin, he condemned sin in the flesh" (Rom. 8:3b). Christ's *active* obedience refers to his meritorious life of law-keeping, whereby he acquires the blessing of eternal life, which Adam forfeited all those years ago.

The net result of Christ's obedience—passive and active— is breathtaking. What is imputed to us is not simply that we are no longer guilty—that's what his *passive* obedience means for us. Christ's passive obedience means that the guilt we

have inherited by Adam—and have increased ourselves—no longer stands against us because Christ suffered the penalty which that guilt required. He suffered the consequences, when he lived in this fallen and sin-seared world, and he suffered the penalty when he drank the cup of divine wrath to the dregs as he hung there on the cross. But his obedience means *more* than simply that we are no longer guilty. His obedience means also that we are *righteous*, and that we have *peace with God* leading to *eternal life*. Those benefits cannot be attributed entirely to the death of Christ—as if death by itself wins them. Rather, they are won by the *life of Christ*. This is his active obedience, whereby he obeys the law of God *perfectly*. The law that Adam broke, and we all broke. This is the law that rendered sinful actions *sinful* from Adam to Moses—the law that we were required to obey by virtue of our being made in the image of God, though we could *never* obey on account of our fallen nature. The obedience that renders Christ's posterity righteous is a complete obedience, inextricably tied not simply to an action here or there, but rather to his *whole life*.

In saying that Christ suffered the consequences of this sin-seared world, I have to hasten the qualification that Christ himself did not assume a fallen or sinful nature. He redeems fallen humanity as a human without himself sinning or falling. The reason has everything to do with the fact that he came in order to restore our corruptible natures to incorruptibility. He unites our corruptible wills to his incorruptible will. Were he himself a fallen man, he could not be the spotless lamb to take away the sins of the world, since "fallen" but "sinless" is an incoherent concept. To desire sin is itself sinful, and Christ was not, and could not, be sinful in any way. Additionally, were Christ to assume a fallen human nature, his death could not be substitutionary,

since he would in a sense be dying for his own inherit guilt.[9] As it is, one of the realities the virgin birth signifies is that the fact that Christ was not inheriting a nature from *Adam*, and was therefore not inheriting Adam's fallenness. Rather, he assumed an unfallen nature in order to be the unfallen fountainhead of life and cleansing and redemption for the fallen humanity that would be incorporated into his lineage.

Related to this affirmation that Christ assumed an unfallen nature is the doctrine of *impeccability*. The doctrine of impeccability denies not only that Christ sinned, but also that he *could* have sinned. This does not mean that his temptations or sufferings were somehow illegitimate, as if Christ's inability to sin renders his temptations some kind of farce. Of course, all this is a deep mystery, especially for sinful creatures like us who tend to project all our fallen human experiences onto Christ. We don't know what it's like to be tempted to sin without ourselves sinfully *desiring* to sin. This does not therefore mean, however, that in order for Christ's temptations to be *real*, he must have desired to sin or that he must have been at real personal risk to sin. Just because these things (i.e., the sinful desire to sin and the temptation to sin) are wed for us in our fallen condition at the experiential level does not mean that they essentially require one another.

Again, Christ's impeccability is mysterious to us, but this does not mean we cannot and should not affirm it logically. In fact, it is a truly logical doctrine. Impeccability is only *illogical* if we forget the doctrine of the hypostatic union. Remember, Christ's human nature is always and only *his*— he, the second person of the Trinity, is the sole subject of his nature. We cannot abstract his human nature from his person. Once we accept this, we must conclude that

---

9. For more on this, see chapter 4.

whatever nature we consider (i.e., either the divine nature he subsists as eternally, or the human nature he assumed in time), the subject of that nature—the *who* of the *what* we are considering—must be perfect. Or, to put it more simply: always remember that *natures don't sin, persons do*. When the Son assumed a human nature, he didn't cease to be perfect when he did so. The human nature of Christ is the human nature of a person who is—and could not possibly be otherwise than—perfect.

And for those of us who have clung to Christ by faith, this perfect life becomes *ours* by union. We are united to him by the Spirit in salvation, such that his perfect death becomes our perfect death and his perfect life becomes our perfect life. This is not a legal fiction—as if God agrees to *pretend* that Christ's merit is ours and our demerits are his. Union with Christ renders all these claims breathtakingly *real*. Paul means no hyperbole when he says, "I have been crucified with Christ. It is no longer I who live, but Christ who lives in me. And the life I now live in the flesh I live by faith in the Son of God, who loved me and gave himself for me" (Gal. 2:20). In Christ, we are *righteous*. In Christ, we have obedience accounted to us—a perfect obedience.

One early Church Father, Gregory of Nazianzus, famously puts the matter in this way: "that which He has not assumed He has not healed."[10] This is the whole reason why he came as a human being—and not just as a grown man, but as a *fertilized egg, an embryo*. The Second Person of the Trinity assumed a human nature to recapitulate humanity. He was redeeming a broken humanity. He was being a whole human for mangled and perverted humans, so that he could give

---

10. Gregory of Nazianzus, "Epistle 101 (Epistle 1 to Cleodonius)", in Schaff and Wace, *A Select Library of the Nicene and Post-Nicene Fathers of the Christian Church*, 7:440.

them his wholeness. He was doing "the human life" right for the first time. This is the human life he grants us in salvation, and the human life we are invited to grow up into as Christians.

All this is why we shouldn't labor to avoid Christological heresies simply to have our "orthodoxy card" stamped and approved. Orthodoxy on these matters safeguards the integrity of the gospel itself. God comes to us to bring us to where he is. God the Trinity, who dwells in inexpressible beatitude—perfect in vitality and delight as Father, Son, and Spirit—makes us to be begraced participants in his holy, infinite, joy. Christ becomes what we are so that we might become what he is: blessed in the infinite ocean of triune love. What the Son is by nature, we become by grace, and this is the case only because of the incarnation. He is heaven on earth: the bridge between the celestial and terranean realms, the true Jacob's Ladder and Holy of Holies. Consider these words from the seventeenth century Reformed theologian, Francis Turretin:

> The work of redemption could not have been performed except by a God-man associating by incarnation the human nature with the divine by an indissoluble bond. For since to redeem us, two things were most especially required – the acquisition of death for satisfaction and victory over the same for the enjoyment of life – our mediator ought to be God-man to accomplish these things: man to suffer, God to overcome; man to receive the punishment we deserved, God to endure and drink it to the dregs; man to acquire salvation for us by dying, God to apply it to us by overcoming; man to become ours by the assumption of flesh, God to make us like himself by the bestowal of the Spirit. This neither man nor God alone could do. For neither could God alone be subject

to death, nor man alone conquer it. Man alone could die for men; God alone could vanquish death.[11]

"For Us Men and for Our Salvation"

Recall the church member I described at the beginning of this chapter. I wonder how you think I ought to have responded to his stark expressions of despair? For my own part, I confess I had rehearsed the response I planned to give, and it was ugly. "I've had it with this brother," I had told myself, "His complaining is just too much. I'm not going to indulge him any longer—he's going to get it from me. It's tough-love time. I'm going to take the gloves off and hold up a mirror so he can see how embarrassed he ought to be." Of course, there does come a time in pastoral counsel situations when—without ever forfeiting the gentle and lowly heart of Christ—rebukes and admonitions ought to be dispensed with frankness and care. Indeed, there may come situations when such a response is actually *the faithful* response to the sentiments this church member expressed to me. But this was not one of those situations. I knew it wasn't one of those situations, in part, because I so wanted it to be. I was not committed to rebuke him in a spirit of resigned obedience to Christ, I was rather eager to indulge the fleshly desire to give him a tongue-lashing. But as I prayed through how to respond, with all the motivation for giving "tough-love" brimming up within me, it seemed as though the Spirit of Christ impressed upon my heart the need to take a different approach. What this brother needed was to avert his eyes away from himself and to revel in the loveliness and worthiness of Christ.

---

11. Francis Turretin, *Institutes of Elenctic Theology*, ed. James T Dennison, trans. George Musgrave Giger (Philippsburg, NJ: P&R Publishing, 1997), 2:XIII.xix.

So, rather than calling attention directly to what this brother should do, I called his attention to the perfections of Christ. I reveled in Christ's active and passive obedience. I reveled in Christ's perfect human will, which never bent to the temptation of sin or fleshly shortcuts, which never held on to grudges or wavered or failed. Christ's will, I reminded him, is *perfect*. His obedience was *perfect*. And it was all *human*, "for us and for our salvation." I then turned this brother's attention to what these perfections mean for him on account of his union with Christ. "His perfect obedience was *for you*. That's *your* perfect righteousness we see sweating drops of blood in the garden. Yes, you failed to resist temptation yesterday—but look here! Look at Christ! See him *succeeding*? See him *obeying* and perfecting *righteousness*? That's all yours in Christ—he did this *for you*. He gives you *that* success and *that* obedience. In Christ, you are perfect. In Christ, God can no sooner be ashamed of you than he could be of Christ."

If you are wondering what happened to this church member, I will only say that this was merely one conversation. It did not transform his life in an instant. The problems that had precipitated to this coffee-shop conversation did not go away when we parted, so this conversation was not a silver bullet, but by God's grace, it was a dose of good medicine. "I'm sorry for my earlier apathy and complaints," he said, as we walked to our separate cars, "I feel *hope* for the first time in a long time." He left with all the same problems, but with hope. What followed were many more conversations—some of which contained a dose of "tough-love" and some of which resemble the gentle reminders I've described here—and by God's grace, he appears to be thriving under the pastoral care of his current pastors.

Of course, there is more to a life of holiness than simply reminding ourselves of the active and passive obedience of Christ. We human beings are, after all, composites of body and soul, and obedience and development of virtue is always hard work and involves the formation of the whole person, by the power of the Spirit. We do not simply remind ourselves of Christ's active and passive obedience and then remain sinfully passive ourselves. But in our Spirit-empowered rigorous pursuit of virtuous obedience to Christ, we never leave behind the meritorious active and passive obedience of Christ, which is rendered ours by the imputation of Christ's righteousness and our union with him. Growing in godliness is nothing if not growing up *into* Christ—our obedience to God involves our walking along the path that Christ has *already* cleared in his obedience. We follow his footsteps.

It is no coincidence that Paul's very next words in Romans—after his consideration of the "tale of two Adams"—are: "What shall we say then? Are we to continue in sin that grace may abound? By no means! How can we who died to sin still live in it" (Rom. 6:1)? Such a bounty of grace invariably raises the question of indulgence in the minds of fallen men. But Paul reminds us that to think of grace that way is to think of grace as those who are *in Adam*, not as those who are in *the Second Adam*. We must never forget to which Adam we belong. We are free because of his active and passive obedience. We are not free *to* sin; we are rather free *from* sin. "Let not sin therefore reign in your mortal body, to make you obey its passions. Do not present your members to sin as instruments for unrighteousness, but present yourselves to God as those who have been brought from death to life, and your members to God as instruments for righteousness" (Rom. 6:12-13). Why? "For sin will have

no dominion over you, since you are not under law but under grace" (Rom. 6:14).

All Christians—like all humanity—are born in Adam. But Christians are also born again *in Christ*. We are a part of a new humanity whose liberation from the enslavement of sin and death has already occurred. That's who we *are*. So *let us live like it*. He became incarnate for nothing less than this, after all. God the Son became man not simply to justify his fellow men in a judicial sense—as glorious as that is—but also to transform man *in himself*. He condescended to us not for the purpose of granting us a "get out hell free" card, which we might then use to dismiss our stagnancy in godliness. No, he condescended to us to bring us to himself. Without ever confusing the Creator-creature distinction— as if we lose our creatureliness and become the timelessly eternal Trinity—there is a sense in which God came to us to *deify* us; to grant us a creaturely share by grace in those qualities of holiness and goodness and life that are his by nature. Again, Maximus puts his finger on this point so well:

> For if he has brought to completion his mystical work of becoming human, having become like us in every way save without sin (cf Heb 4:15), and even descended into the lower regions of the earth where the tyranny of sin compelled humanity, then God will also completely fulfill the goal of his mystical work of deifying humanity in every respect, of course, short of an identity of essence with God; and he will assimilate humanity to himself and elevate us to a position above all the heavens.[12]

Let us, as we marvel at the loveliness of Christ's perfect life, by the power of the Spirit, become increasingly who we are. Let us grow up into the righteousness that has been freely given to us by our Jesus, which he has acquired with

---

12. Maximus, *On the Cosmic Mystery of Jesus Christ*, p. 116.

his active and passive obedience. And let us remain ever transfixed by the beauty of his perfect life.

* * *

Lord Jesus Christ, what could we say? We are speechless when we consider your matchless beauty, and the irresistible loveliness of your perfect life. "Thank you" falls woefully short. In Adam, we were powerless and weak and disobedient and rebellious. Yet, you did not leave us in such a dreadful position. You took on a nature capable of achieving all the obedience we owed but could never render. And you did so. "For us men, and for our salvation," you did so. Grant us, by your Spirit, the grace to see your perfect and immutable glory revealed in the beautiful life of a perfect human nature. Forbid, Lord, that we should ever grow cold or indifferent to the active and passive obedience with which you grant us, and may we grow up in that obedience freely given, so that we might resemble your lovely life increasingly forevermore. Amen.

4

Atonement

A Misunderstood Doctrine

I will never forget the sense of shock I felt as I listened to an address at a pastor's conference some years ago. At the time, I was working and studying at a seminary, and my attendance at the conference was part of my job. It was a pretty sweet deal for the seminarian who was all-to-eager to take up any opportunity to attend conferences for free. Setting up and manning a table with promotional material for the seminary I represented was a small price to pay for free admission to some of the best Bible teaching in the world, with access to some of the best curated conference-bookstores. Not a small portion of my library right now can be traced back to this time as a seminary employee, working the conference circuit around the U.S. But at this particular conference, the speaker left me positively dumbstruck. He was speaking on the atonement, and in typical Baptist homiletic fashion, he had steadily built up to a thundering crescendo. Slamming his fist on the sturdy pulpit, in front of no less than a thousand attendees, he bellowed out his point: "The death of Jesus didn't save anyone; the death of Jesus made salvation *possible*!" He struck the syllables of that last

word for emphasis. "*Po-ssi-ble!*" From a pastoral standpoint, I could not fathom how the preacher imagined he was delivering a celebratory word. Something to elicit praise of God and comfort for the needy Christian. *That's it? Christ came to live and die and rise to make salvation possible?*

Notwithstanding my vehement disagreement, I'm grateful for this address. The honest starkness of his declaration does us a great service. Such a statement, after all, *accurately* depicts what most evangelicals believe about Christ's death, even if most of us would want to put a better spin on it. We'd prefer to call it "universal" atonement, which sounds more inclusive, and contrasts nicely with the alternative "limited" atonement, which sounds, well, *limiting.* Universal atonement sounds better because it apparently bespeaks a generosity on Christ's part—a generosity that is intuitively welcome to most of us. "Christ made atonement for *everyone*—anyone can get in on it with the exercise of their free will. Come and receive this free gift!" But whatever spin we place on it, such vision of the atonement is precisely what the aforementioned preacher portrayed. Rather than calling it a "universal" atonement, it would be far more accurate to call it a "possible" atonement.

Proponents of such a view are not likely to be as enthusiastic as the preacher from my story, however, since the alternative to a "possible atonement" would be something like, "definite atonement." But I think this is *exactly* the right contrast (possible atonement vs. definite atonement), and in this chapter, I intend to revel in the beauty of Christ's efficacious, definite atonement. Our Beautiful Shepherd lays his life down for his sheep in an act of unparalleled care (John 10:14-18). Our Beautiful Bridegroom lays his life down for his Bride in an act of sacrificial devotion (Eph. 5:25-28). Our Beautiful High Priest performs his duties flawlessly (Heb. 5:10). Our Beautiful Lamb is willingly slain to make atonement for

people from every tribe and tongue and nation (Rev. 5:8-10). In all of this, we should labor to ensure that our thundering point about Christ's death is *not* that "the death of Jesus made salvation *possible*," but rather the confident declaration that "a death has occurred that *redeems*" (Heb. 9:15), since "by a single offering *he has perfected* for all time those who are being sanctified" (Heb. 10:14).

Holiness, Love, and Wrath

God is holy, and God is love. There is no competition between these two claims, they are one in the same because (as we saw in Chapter 1), God is *simple*. He is pure act—he is himself wholly and has no parts or passions. In considering God's being, God *is* his holiness, and he *is* his love, and his love *is* his holiness. Crucially, we must understand that God's attributes don't balance each other out. He never lets off a little of his holiness so that he can express some of his love, and vice versa. Everything he is and does is supremely loving and holy.

Since God loves purely, and he is that which is most supremely worthy of love, God loves himself purely, and his love for himself is a white-hot fire of holiness. He supremely approves of that which is Good, and he must therefore disapprove of that which is opposed to that which is Good. This means that God's wrath is not a divine attribute, properly speaking. To be sure, the Scriptures speak without a hint of hesitation about God's wrath. He himself has inspired the declaration that "he is a righteous judge, and a God who feels indignation every day" (Ps. 7:11; see also Rom. 1:18-31). Where the Scriptures speak emphatically, we should gladly do so as well. However, we have not spoken clearly of the Scriptures if we present their contents as if they are self-contradictory. Whatever we say about God's wrath,

it must accord with what we say of his divine simplicity and his aseity, which we examined in Chapter 1. God must be simple in the sense that he is not comprised of parts. If he were composed in that way, God would have to depend on not-God for God to be God (i.e., whatever unifying principle brings the composite parts of God together). The God who depends on not-God to be God is *not* the God of the Bible.

While we can maintain that "love" and "holiness" are true attributes of God because they are not "parts" of him but are rather ways of describing the one simple divine nature, we cannot say the same thing about divine "wrath." Why? Because God's wrath is something that requires an *object* apart from himself. He does not feel wrath towards himself, after all, for nothing could be *less holy* than feeling wrath toward the Almighty, all-holy, all-loving one! So, God's wrath does not exist in the abstract or with reference to his own nature, but rather only toward sin. This being the case, wrath *cannot* be a divine attribute—an attribute that defines God *as* God. Were this the case, we would have to conclude, absurdly, that God is not truly and fully himself until he has sinners to feel indignation toward.

How, then, should we think of God's wrath? Is it a figment of our imagination? Is it a biblical lie? No, rather, divine wrath (which is *not* a divine attribute) is nothing other than the expression of divine holiness and divine love (which *are* divine attributes). As the one who is all-loving, he loves that which is supremely Good, and must punish that which disapproves of supreme Goodness. As the one who is perfectly holy, he cannot but consume that which is unholy. When we see God's wrath on display, in other words, we are seeing a fitting and righteous and glorious expression of God's love and holiness—such a display is the only truly loving and holy one in the face of sin. To say that

God has wrath is to accommodate God's actions for human understanding by using human emotive language. When we punish, we often feel wrath, therefore, to teach us that God punishes sin and administers justice against law-breaking, Holy Scripture speaks of his "wrath."

This principle is something each of us can intuit at some level. Profound love for my wife and children begets motivation to *act* at the prospect of their harm at the hands of a malicious attacker. I might even say I feel *indignation* at that prospect. Moving beyond this relatable level, however, is difficult for those of us who live East of Eden. It is simple enough to understand the issue when the crime is an attack and the one harmed is someone close to us, but it is much more difficult to understand the "indignation" God feels "everyday." Even more difficult for us to comprehend is that this "daily indignation" is a kind altogether different from the kind of indignation we feel as creatures tainted by sin, in the sense that his is not "impassioned" like ours always is. Again, this is a form of accommodated speech: God is changeless in his state of beatitude, his state of rest. But his execution of justice and punishment against sin has to be communicated to creatures like us, who are fundamentally impassioned creatures. He does that by inspiring words like "indignation." But we must always remember that the analogy flows in one direction: we cannot take experiences of our indignation and project that back up onto God just because the word is used, as if God is inviting us to "sympathize" with him at all. This needle is incredibly hard to thread: to accept the accommodated language God gives us in Holy Scripture without projecting our own creaturely experiences of that language back up into God. We don't even understand the idea of "non-impassioned indignation"—for us, to feel indignation is to be *moved* by something external

to us. Indignation is the passionate *reaction* we feel in the face of (perceived or actual) evil. But God is not a composite of parts *or passions*—which means his unchanging nature applies even to this idea of "indignation." He is not *moved* to feel indignation by something external to him, for that would mean that he has something like an "emotional state" that is subject to (dare I say, even *held hostage to*) something or someone outside of himself. He would need for something to move his emotional state so as to feel rightly.

What a dreadful thought!

On the contrary, God's unchangeable nature (his immutability) implies a lack of change and subjectivity to what he "feels." This expression of changelessness is the divine attribute of *impassibility*, and it should inform the way we think about the Bible's description of divine wrath. It means that when we see the Scriptures speaking of God showing forth his wrath, we are not seeing a God who flies off the handle and loses self-control. Rather, we are seeing a God of perfect self-happiness expressing his divine love and holiness toward sin in the most righteous, most loving, and most holy way imaginable. We are seeing, in other words, the fire of divine holiness do what it does: *burn*. The fire that purifies gold destroys its imperfections and dross—to affirm one *is* to affirm the other.

Why am I saying all of this? Because if we don't get these matters straight, we will badly misunderstand what's happening in the gospel. We can come to imagine that the cross is where divine love and divine wrath compete with one another, with divine love being the triumphant victor. But this is a gross misrepresentation of the gospel. Rather, the glorious mystery of the gospel is that God's wrath—as a perfect expression of holiness and love—truly consumes the sin it must consume without destroying its perpetrators.

Sidebar 4.1
Divine Simplicity

This doctrine affirms that God is not comprised in any way. He is not a composite of material and immaterial existence, nor is he composed of immaterial or metaphysical "parts." He is not the composition of potential and actualized potential, nor is he the sum total of his parts, nor any other thing at all. This doctrine is true because of other divine attributes, e.g. God's *aseity* (i.e., the doctrine that affirms that God is *of himself* or *self-sufficient*) and God's *immutability* or *changelessness* (i.e., the doctrine that affirms that God does not and cannot change in any way, since he is perfect in himself). If God were the composite of various attributes or parts that are not identical with God's essence, his existence would be *dependent* on these attributes or parts, which would mean that God is dependent on not-God in order to be God and does therefore not have *aseity.* This doctrine has been historically crucial for articulating and defending the doctrine of the Trinity. The three persons of the Trinity are not *parts* of the simple divine essence, but are rather subsistences of the one, simple, divine nature.

Out of love for himself and his holiness, he pours out divine wrath on our sin. And out of that same love for himself and his holiness, he reconciles us to himself so that we might be made recipients of his holy love without being utterly consumed. How is it possible for God to do both? How is it possible for God to manifest his holiness and love by pouring out his wrath on my sin *while also* manifesting his holiness and love by reconciling me to him and making me a recipient of his holy love? Answer: the most beautiful sacrifice made by the most beautiful man, Jesus Christ. To this grand mystery we shall now turn.

Propitiation and Substitution

In Paul's letter to the Romans, he is concerned, in part, with describing, defining, and reveling in the gospel. The

exquisite gospel. But before he can describe the good news of what God does to save man from his sin, he must describe the bad news of human sin and depravity, and the wrath of God it demands (for the bad news of sin and depravity and wrath are what make the good news of the exquisite gospel *good*). Paul must first spread out the silky, pitch black backdrop of sin and its effects so that the brilliance of the "gospel-diamond" can be clearly seen by contrast. That leg of Paul's argument begins in Romans 1:18 ("For the wrath of God is revealed from heaven against all ungodliness and unrighteousness of men ...") and is sustained until 3:20 ("For by works of the law no human being will be justified in his sight, since through the law comes knowledge of sin"). Paul's description of the plight of sin reaches its apex in Romans 3:9-12: "For we have already charged that *all,* both Jews and Greeks, are under sin, as it is written: None is righteous, no, not one; no one understands; no one seeks for God. All have turned aside; together they have become worthless; no one does good, not even one." The Gentiles are doomed. The Jews are doomed. The wrath of God is revealed from heaven against all ungodliness, and that ungodliness is universally pervasive.

Having laid out the silky backdrop, Paul is now prepared, in 3:21ff, to present the brilliant, exquisite "gospel-diamond" for our admiration. Here is the most crucial turning point in all the book of Romans. In making this turn, Paul is also resolving the problem that the preceding chapters have created—the mystery of God's holiness and love and wrath in relation to the reconciliation of sinners to himself. The point in the preceding chapters of Romans was to show God's righteousness in judging sin, so that "every mouth may be stopped, and the whole world may be held accountable to God" (Rom. 3:19). But you see, Paul was so effective in

making this point that *now* the question changes. No longer must Paul answer, "How could God be just in *condemning* everyone?" Having argued so convincingly, *now* the question has become, "How could God be just in *justifying* anyone?" Given how wicked the whole world is, how can God rightly set his love on *anyone*? How can anyone be acquitted when everyone justly deserves death and hell?

Paul's answer is breathtaking. "But now the righteousness of God has been manifested apart from the law, although the Law and the prophets bear witness to it—the righteousness of God through faith in Jesus Christ for all who believe" (Rom. 3:21-22). Paul picks up on the point he left off in verse twenty, "For by works of the law no human being will be justified in God's sight," and so it should make sense that "the righteousness of God has been manifested *apart from the law*." However, as Paul will go on to explain in 7:7-13, this does not imply a deficiency on the law's part. The law was never *intended* to justify human beings. The righteousness of God was always intended to be manifested apart from the law, and the Law and the Prophets—i.e., the whole Old Testament—bear witness to this fact. The law announces, as it were, "Obedience to me does not justify. I bring knowledge of sin without directly giving you its solution. But I anticipate a righteousness of God that will be manifested *apart from* me."

We will return to this idea of the relationship between the Old Testament and the gospel momentarily, but first we need to deal with this phrase, "the righteousness of God." Much ink has been spilled over this phrase. What does Paul mean by it? There are many different takes on this, but broadly speaking, commentators divide into two categories. The first insist the "righteousness of God" is God's own moral perfection. The "righteousness *of* God" is "God's own righteousness," his

own judicial and ethical uprightness—his essential inability to work injustice. This would include his trustworthiness, and covenant faithfulness; his perfect track record to do what he says and be true to the covenants into which he enters with his people. The second option is to think about God's "righteousness" as his "saving righteousness." That is, his active intentionality to save sinners. This would include the notion of "imputed" righteousness—a righteousness that God gives to people out of grace in saving them. So, which is it? Are we talking about "the righteousness that *belongs to* God," or "the righteousness that *comes from* God?" The answer is "both."

I believe Paul uses a phrase that has the capacity for versatility *on purpose*. This whole book uses "the righteousness of God" in a variety of ways. You could say that Paul intends to show how God is righteous, to righteously save, by imputing Christ's righteousness to those who would have him by faith. In fact, verse 26 makes this point crystal clear: "It was to show his *righteousness* at the present time, so that he might be *just*"—i.e., the righteousness that belongs to God—"and the *justifier*"—i.e., the righteousness that *comes from* God. And this saving righteousness comes "through faith in Jesus Christ for all who believe." *That* is how this righteousness is appropriated: faith in Jesus Christ.

Don't miss the sweeping claim Paul makes here in this passage. According to Paul, this is the only way God saves anyone: by giving them righteousness through faith in Jesus Christ. They bring the empty hands of faith to Jesus, and in receiving Jesus they receive righteousness. This is the case, Paul says, for everyone who wishes to be saved, "For there is no distinction: for all have sinned and fall short of the glory of God" (Rom. 3:22b-23). What does it mean to fall short of God's glory? Paul has already told us in Romans 1:21:

"For although they knew God, they did not honor him as God or give thanks to him, but they became futile in their thinking and their foolish hearts were darkened." To fall short of God's glory is a failure to recognize God's all-importance and insist on rendering the worship due him to lesser objects (Rom. 1:22-23). All of us—Jew or Gentile, black or white, rich or poor, man or woman, child or parent—are condemned in our first father Adam the same way: we sin and fall short of the glory of God. And everyone who is saved—Jew or Gentile, black or white, rich or poor, man or woman, child or parent—is saved the same way: we are "justified by his grace as a gift, through the redemption that is in Christ Jesus" (Rom. 3:24).

Now, this term "justified" brings up the notion of God's righteousness again. "Justification," as we considered in the previous chapter, is a legal term—a declaration that one is not guilty and in right standing before God. Paul says that those who are "justified"—who are declared righteous—have this declaration pronounced over them "by his grace as a gift." God's declaration that a sinner is justified, Paul says, is a gift. We don't earn it; we receive it. If we wish to be declared "not-guilty," we must receive that verdict as a gift; we can't work off our debt of guilt. That is, we may receive it as a gift, or we will not receive it at all.

But again, if this is so, how can God remain just? The sinner whom God acquits in the act of justification, in himself, does not deserve acquittal. Rather, he deserves death and hell. How can God remain just if he does not render the penalty due? How can he be "the just" while also being "the justifier?" We get at answer to this question when we consider how God justifies man. Namely, by putting "Christ forward as a propitiation by his blood, to be received by faith" (Rom. 3:25). What does that mean? The word "propitiation"

relates to the satisfaction of divine wrath. Christ being a "propitiation" means that God's wrath against sin was satisfied. Now, some people find this objectionable because they think it implies God the Father stands above humanity, eager to pour out his wrath, and the Son stands in our stead and forces the Father to reluctantly show mercy to us. But there is no divide in the persons of the Trinity here. It is not the case that God the Father hates sin and sinners, while Christ loves the sinner, and thereby offers "propitiation" to satisfy God's wrath on our behalf. It was *God*, after all, who *put Christ* forward as a propitiation. He provided for himself his own means to show mercy to sinners. Indeed, the act of propitiation is itself a Trinitarian act. Recall what we said earlier about inseparable operations: the external works of the Trinity are undivided. It is the wrath of God the Trinity that Christ is absorbing as the perfect God-man. God saves us by propitiating his own wrath himself in the person of the Word-made-flesh. The cross is not the work of the Son alone, but is rather the work of the Trinity.

Sidebar 4.2
Inseparable Operations

This doctrine affirms that the external works of the Trinity are undivided. Since God is undivided, the actions of God are undivided. The persons of the Trinity never act independently of one another—all the works of the Trinity are *trinitarian*. Since God is *Father, Son, and Spirit,* all that God does is accomplished *from* the Father, *through* the Son, and *by* the Spirit. Therefore, when we see persons of the Trinity accomplishing divine works in the story of redemption, we must not separate them from one another as if each person has their own independent actions. All God's works— even when appropriated to one person especially more explicitly than another—are the accomplishments of the Trinity, and the Trinity should therefore receive our praise for any divine action in question.

But there is more to this language of God "putting Christ forward as a propitiation by his blood, to be received by faith." The language of propitiation does not simply appeal to the notion of satisfying "wrath," it does so more specifically within the Old Testament context of atonement. The clearest Old Testament picture of atonement is found in Leviticus 16, where we find the Day of Atonement described. This was the most important day of the year, because it was the day in which the high priest of Israel would offer atonement for the sins of the people as a form of covenant renewal with God. The day was very elaborate, and involved the concepts of cleansing and expiation, where the sins of the people were *removed,* and where the stain of sin was *cleansed* by blood, and most importantly, the sins of the people were *punished* in the substitutionary sacrifice of animals. That blood was taken into the most holy place in the tabernacle—the place where God dwells in his unapproachable glory, where *the mercy seat* was located—and *propitiation was offered there.* The priest would sprinkle the blood on the mercy seat and would appeal to God's mercy with it. He would, in effect, say, "Lord, this people is guilty. But receive this blood sacrifice in *their* stead."

So, when Paul says in Romans 3 that *God put forward Christ as a propitiation by his blood, to be received by faith,* for *all* who believe, without distinction, he is saying something truly remarkable. In the gospel, God took that mercy seat, which only the high priest saw, and *only* once a year, when he offered sacrifices *only* for the people of Israel, and brought it out for anyone and everyone to receive redemption and justification. What was once hidden by veils and sealed off only to the nation of Israel has now been taken out of the holy of holies and placed right there in the open air for anyone to receive its atonement by faith. Now atonement is no longer

simply available to the few; it has been made available to the many—Jew and Gentile.

And what do we find when we—the masses—come and approach that mercy seat that God has placed within our reach? We find Jesus, the spotless Lamb of God, who suffered as a substitute. *We* sin and fall short of God's glory, and so God has *wrath*. For Christ to be the propitiation to be received by faith means that when we receive him by faith, he satisfies the wrath of God *on our behalf*. And this is how he justifies! Justification—that legal declaration that we are *not guilty* and are now *righteous*—cannot be accomplished if our sins are not accounted for.

The reason God can be just whilst justifying sinners is that they whom he justifies have had their sins *justly punished* in Christ. There has never been, nor will there ever be, an unpunished sin. All sin is punished in hell or on the cross. Incidentally, this point is difficult to square with a notion of universal atonement. If Christ died to atone for each and every sin that has ever been committed, why does *anyone* go to hell? Wouldn't universal atonement demand universal salvation? Some will say that people go to hell simply on account of their unbelief. But this is just an attempt to kick the can down the road a bit longer. Is such unbelief not a sin? If so, is it not a sin for which Christ has paid with his universal atonement?

In any case, my present concern is to emphasize that no sin ever goes unpunished. *Ever.* This means that no one experiences forgiveness from God because God *ignores* their sin. *He cannot do that.* Anyone who experiences forgiveness from God experiences that forgiveness because God punished their sins in Christ. Even those saints in the Old Testament. Their *sins too* were punished at the cross of Christ. Did you notice that at the end of verse 25? "This"—i.e., God putting

Christ forward as a propitiation to be received by faith—"was to show God's righteousness, because in his divine forbearance he had *passed over former sins.*" So evidently, with Old Testament atonement, God wasn't dealing with sin in an ultimate sense; he was rather *passing over* them. This, incidentally, is why God's righteousness is manifested *apart* from the law. If the law shows God *passing over* former sins, God's righteousness with respect to those sins is still in question. What happens to those sins that he passes over? What happens to the sins of faithless Israel? Of Moses, or David, or Nehemiah? Are they freebies? Does God let their sins slide? If so, he could not be righteous. But he doesn't pass over former sins forever. This "passing over" in former times "was to show his righteousness *at the present time*, so that he might be just and the justifier of the one who has faith in Jesus" (Rom. 3:26).

God's righteousness, in other words, wasn't shown with respect to sin *back then*—when he was passing over former sins—but rather, his righteousness is shown *at the present time*—now that Christ has arrived, and the mercy seat has been brought out into the open, and propitiation has been offered, and wrath has been satisfied on account of the blood of Christ. So, what happened to the sins of Moses and David and Nehemiah—those sins that God formerly passed over? Answer: *they were punished in the death of Jesus Christ.* God was not passing over them to leave them unpunished, he was passing over them *until the present time*, when he could demonstrate his righteousness by paying for them in the death of Christ.

You see, every saint in all human history is saved in the exact same way. They are saved by the grace of God through faith alone in Christ alone. Old Testament saints who had *no idea* that there would be a Nazarene carpenter named

Jesus Christ were saved by faith in that Nazarene carpenter on account of his death without knowing him. How can this be the case? *They had faith that God would provide* (see Gen. 22:14; Ps. 19:12). They had faith in God to provide a means of justification—to declare them innocent. They didn't know *how* he would do it in all of its historically specific contours, but they had faith *that* he would do it. Further, saints in the Old Testament had every indication that God would provide this justification by means of some kind of *penal substitution* (i.e., it would be legal—concurrent with God's righteous requirements of the law—and it would be substitutionary—someone or something would suffer the consequences of sin on their behalf). Penal substitutionary atonement is signaled to as far back as Genesis 3:21, when God fashioned garments with animal skins (presumably, animals that had to be *killed* and *skinned*) to cover Adam and Eve's shame of nakedness. This substitutionary pattern is repeated in Genesis 22:1-14—where we read about the ram dying in the place of Isaac—Exodus 12:1-32—where the angel of Death passes over those homes in Israel whose doorposts are painted with the blood of a lamb that was slain on their behalf—Leviticus 16—where we read about the Day of Atonement, described above—and Isaiah 52:13–53:12—where we are told of Yahweh's suffering servant who would be "pierced for our transgressions" and "crushed for our iniquities." All these and more were shadows of the substantive atoning sacrifice that Christ would offer at Calvary.

And we, on this side of the cross, look back and say with confidence, "That's what Abraham received by faith. He received the atonement Christ *would* offer! And that's what *we* receive by faith. We receive the atonement Christ *did* offer!" Everyone before the incarnation was looking ahead to a blurry vision of God's redemption, but since Christ has

come, the picture has sharpened. What was blurry for them is clear for us: all fall short of the glory of God and those who are justified are justified by his grace as a gift, through the redemption that is in Christ Jesus.

Definite Atonement

All that we have said thus far has significant implications for our earlier claim that the death of Christ does not merely make salvation *possible*, but rather *actually saves*. Consider the nature of Christ's intercessory work. The work of Jesus in the atonement is part of a particular office that he holds; namely, that of the Great High Priest. The book of Hebrews spends a great deal of space describing how Jesus fulfills the corresponding responsibilities of earthly priests in greater ways. We are told that he is superior in that his priesthood participates in a better covenant (Heb. 7:22), is eternal and not limited by death (Heb. 7:23-24), and involves a single sacrifice, which sufficiently accomplished what earthly priests could never accomplish with their multitude of sacrifices (Heb. 10:11-12). We could certainly go on, but the manner of his superiority I wish to consider right now is the effectiveness of his intercessory work.

The author of Hebrews writes, "The former priests were many in number, because they were prevented by death from continuing in office, but he holds his priesthood permanently, because he continues forever. Consequently, he is able to save to the uttermost those who draw near to God through him, since he always lives to make intercession for them" (Heb. 7:23-24). Here, it is vital that we keep in mind the relationship between the atoning sacrifice offered by a priest, and that priest's intercession for the people. It is the offering that *qualifies* the intercession "… the priests go regularly into the first section … but into the second only the high priest goes, and he but once a year, and *not*

without blood, which he offers for himself and for the unintentional sins of the people" (Heb. 9:6-7). This is the idea: the offering is made on behalf of those for whom the priest intercedes. In other words, Jesus intercedes for those he died for. Everyone whose sins were atoned for receives the intercession of Christ's priestly office. His intercession and his death are inseparable. Furthermore, Hebrews 7:24 says that the effect of Jesus' intercession is *salvation to the uttermost*, which rules out the possibility that Jesus is interceding for non-believers, which would necessarily follow if his atonement was meant to deal with their sins. Universal atonement would mean universal intercession, which could result in nothing other than universal salvation because his intercession is always effective. If Jesus offers an atoning sacrifice to pay for the sins of a non-believer, and thereafter does *not* intercede for that non-believer, then his priestly work is *incomplete* (and he therefore is in no position to *sit down*. See Heb. 1:3; Heb. 10:12).

The author of Hebrews goes on to make this point of Christ's efficacious atonement when he writes, "But when Christ had offered for all time a single sacrifice for sins, he sat down at the right hand of God, waiting from that time until his enemies should be made a footstool for his feet. For by a single offering he has perfected for all time those who are being sanctified" (Heb. 10:12-14). Note, it was by the offering that he has perfected those who are being sanctified. The author does not write that by a single offering, "he has offered perfection" or "has made perfection possible," but rather that by a single offering, he "has perfected." See the glorious grace of Christ's High Priestly work: he is the Great High Priest who offers a perfect sacrifice, and he is the perfect Sacrifice itself. He is spotless in his life, to make him a fitting substitute, and he is spotless in his priestly service, to make him a High Priest superior to any before him.

The Particularity of Love

Not only is definite atonement clearly taught in Scripture, it also rhymes with what we know to be true from our own experiences in this world. To illustrate, consider the following contrast between two very different fictional characters from two very different novels. First, consider Ivan Karamazov, of Dostoevsky's masterpiece, *The Brothers Karamazov*. Ivan, if you are unfamiliar with this tale, is a disenchanted, disillusioned atheist, who objects to the faith of his brother, Alyosha, chiefly on the grounds of the problem of evil. In one particularly crucial episode in the novel, we are to picture Alyosha sitting opposite his brother Ivan at a café, where they discuss Ivan's philosophy of life. Here, Alyosha finds himself unable to give a response to the onslaught of questions regarding the justice of God in allowing—nay, *ordaining*—so much suffering in this world. "Listen," says Ivan, "if everyone has to suffer in order to bring about eternal harmony through that suffering, tell me, please, what have the children to do with this? It's quite incomprehensible that they too should have to suffer, that they too should have to pay for harmony by their suffering. Why should they be the grist to someone else's mill?"[1] This question—the *problem of evil*, as it's called—is not new, and many an inquirer has similarly concluded with Ivan in skepticism and a rejection of an absolutely good God. Of course, in doing so, they land with Ivan in a nihilistic bind in which their objection to God not only justifies unbelief in God, but also leads to the self-defeat of their original objections. Like a snake devouring its own tail, such doubt can only conclude with Ivan's axiom: "If God does not exist, then all things are permissible," in

---

1. Fyodor Dostoevsky, *The Brothers Karamazov*, trans. Ignat Avsey, 1a ed. 1980; reimpr. 2008 (Oxford, UK: Oxford University Press, 2011), p. 306.

which case the moral outrage that eventuated in God's denial becomes one more "thing permissible." There is no more moral standard by which to object to God's falling short for Ivan, by the time he is finished logic-chopping. With God out of the picture, so too goes moral objectivity, and the problem of evil becomes no problem at all. "All things"— including the suffering of children—"are permissible."

But I share this story about Ivan and his morally suicidal logic not to point out the self-defeating nature of the problem of evil as it is articulated by those hostile to God, but rather to highlight the apparently noble alternative that Ivan offers. In the crescendo of his monologue, Ivan declares this manifesto:

> I want forgiveness, I want to embrace everyone, I want an end to suffering. And if the suffering of children is required to make up the total suffering necessary to attain the truth, then I say here and now that no truth is worth such a price... I don't want harmony; for the love of humankind, I don't want it. I would rather that suffering were not avenged. I would prefer to keep my suffering unavenged and my abhorrence unplacated, *even at the risk of being wrong.* Besides, the price of harmony has been set too high, we can't afford the entrance fee. And that's why I hasten to return my entry ticket. If I ever want to call myself an honest man, I have to hand it back as soon as possible. And that's exactly what I'm doing. It's not that I don't accept God, Alyosha; I'm just with the utmost respect, handing Him back my ticket.[2]

Notice how high and noble Ivan sounds. Ivan recognizes his reasoning may conclude in rational absurdity, but he believes to embrace such a view is to take the moral high ground. He is, in his own estimation, *more* just and *more loving to humanity* than God seems to be. The irony is that

---

2. Dostoyevsky, *The Brothers Karamazov*, pp. 307-8.

Ivan, as a character within this novel, seems to be the most incapable of loving even a single *person*. Opining about love for *humanity* comes naturally to Ivan, so long as humanity remains an indefinite mass—a hypothetical. Ivan would do anything for humanity—he would *die* for humanity. But would he inconvenience himself for even a single person? Not likely. For individuals, Ivan has nothing but contempt. If only the individuality of humanity as it is could conform to Ivan's ideals of humanity in the hypothetical, he would be the most noble character in Dostoyevsky's novel. But, alas, the stubborn reality of individuals as individuals keeps Ivan loving everyone in theory, and no one in reality.

Contrast the idealism of Ivan Karamazov with the startling realism of Noel Crowe, the protagonist of Niall Williams' wonderful novel, *This is Happiness*. In this novel, Noel narrates one particular year in the small Irish parish of Faha in 1958. As an old man, Noel reflects on his past self—the seventeen-year-old seminary drop-out—having just fallen in love for the very first time. Here is his epiphany:

> I had no understanding yet that in this life the greatest predicament of man and womankind was just how to love another person. You knew in your blood it was the right thing, you knew somehow without ever having had a single lesson, without it ever being mentioned once in thirteen years of school, without your mother or father saying the word out loud once you passed the age of four and went in short trousers to the nuns whose only use, not to say knowledge of it, was in reference to God, so it seemed both supreme and unreal at the same time, and lived in an aura of aspiration, a place inside you that aspired up in a spire nearer to heaven maybe, and not the actual ground of dirt and puddles and broken pavement you and your heel-broke shoes lived on. You knew, you knew the Commandments, had learned them out of the missal-thin pages of the green

Catechism, where, in a genius move of utter simplicity God had set the high bar for Christianity by saying *Love your neighbour like yourself,* and you read that and looked over at your neighbour, Patrick Plunkett picking his nose and pressing the pickings on the underside of your desk, and by virtue of nothing more than carnal reality that bar got that much higher. Still, *you knew,* you knew that the purpose of human beings was to love, just that, and though you knew it, though it was maybe the only given in the ceaseless search for purpose, the evidence of the perplex of love was all around you, so that though there were weddings and white dresses and roses, though every song was a love-song, there were black eyes and bitter words and crying babies too, and every heart got broken sometime, yet, and yet, and yet still again, because you couldn't deny it, because, if anything was, it was a fundament, it was in the first intention, part of the first motion when the first key was wound and the whole clockwork of man and woman was first set going, love was where everyone was trying to get to.[3]

What Ivan doesn't understand is that to love *everyone* in the abstract is to love *no one* in reality—but what Noel came to realize is that the commandment to love humanity at all is fulfilled in the impossible task of truly loving just *one person.* The question cannot be avoided: "Who is my neighbor" (Luke 10:29)? And we can never escape the answer: *that one.* Patrick Plunkett. Sophie Troy. Ivan Karamazov. Your enemy. Your friend. The individual who stands before you. This command, to love one's neighbor, though universal, is impossible to fulfill in the abstract. *It is impossible to fulfill strictly at the level of the universal.* The command to love one's neighbor is stubbornly concrete and forces you to confront this fixed and unbending reality: love is particular,

---

3. Niall Williams, *This Is Happiness* (London, UK: Bloomsbury, 2019), pp. 220-1.

or it is not love at all. Therefore, the particularity of Christ's love in the atonement—the fact that he lays his life down *for his Bride*, for *his flock*, for his own people, with names and faces and objectionable personalities and problems—is marvelously good news. The particularity of the atonement, in other words, makes the atonement a truly loving act. It is the display of love at its highest manifestation.

Christus Victor

The atoning death of Christ does not only result in the forgiveness of our sins and the propitiation of divine wrath. The death of Christ—with his resurrection—also accomplishes *victory* over Satan and the demonic powers of darkness. This aspect of Christ's atoning work is sometimes portrayed as another—or as a *competing*—"theory" of the atonement, set over and against the "penal substitutionary" atonement I've just described above. But this is not a very helpful characterization. Granted, it's not uncommon at all for evangelicals to describe the atonement of Christ without any mention to this aspect of Christ's victory over the devil (or, *Christus Victor*). Because of this, the discovery of *Christus Victor* is received as a breath of fresh air to many an evangelical, who see it replete throughout the tradition of Christianity. Since its doctrinal appeal is (rightly) undeniable, and since it is often (wrongly) advertised as an alternative to penal substitution, some evangelicals might be tempted to forfeit substitution, while *other* evangelicals, in response, might be tempted to view *Christus Victor* with suspicion. Neither of these reactions are right, because these aspects of Christ's atonement are fully compatible. In fact, we can even go so far as to say they *require* one another.

The most basic place we see these two glorious atonement-realities interact with one another is Colossians 2:13-15, where

Paul writes, "And you, who were dead in your trespasses and the uncircumcision of your flesh, God made alive together with him, having forgiven us all our trespasses, by canceling the record of debt that stood against us with its legal demands. This he set aside, nailing it to the cross. He disarmed the rulers and authorities and put them to open shame, by triumphing over them in him." Satan's vocation is *accusation*. His primary power over humanity is the threat of Death in light of God's wrath—Death + divine wrath = Hell. He loves for nothing more than to watch people suffer under the just condemnation of God. So, when he accuses, it is like he is trying to leverage God's own righteousness against us. He acts as prosecutor. He goes before God with all our list of sins, and he reads them, one by one, and says, "There you have it. They are guilty! It is time to send them to the fiery pit." But in dying on the cross, the Lord Jesus robs Satan of any means of accusation. The threat of Satan and death depend on our sins. His plan is to condemn us before God, so that death might be our doorway to hell. But because Christ has taken our record of debt that stood against us with his legal demands, and has set it aside—nailing it to the cross—we who trust in Christ have had our sins removed, the threat of hell is taken off the table, death is defanged, and Satan is humiliated. In other words, penal substitution is *how* Christ has victory over Satan.

Now, as a defeated foe, the best he can do to justified saints is cause them to despair because of their sin—to cause them to doubt the victorious work of Christ's penal substitutionary atonement. Which means, gaining victory over the devil's influence in our lives never involves minimizing Christ's substitutionary work, but rather throwing it back at his face! Martin Luther got this point powerfully when he wrote this in a letter to a friend struggling with a tender conscience:

When the devil throws our sins up to us and declares that we deserve death and hell, we ought to speak thus: "I admit that I deserve death and hell. What of it? Does this mean that I shall be sentenced to eternal damnation? By no means. For I know One who suffered and made satisfaction in my behalf. His name is Jesus Christ, the Son of God. Where he is, there I shall be also."[4]

He Descended to the Dead

While I can only afford to say so much about this contested topic here, we should consider briefly an oft neglected aspect of Christ's death on the cross: his descent to Hades.[5] The completion of Christ's humiliation *and* the beginning of Christ's exaltation is when he descends to the grave after his death. This is what we confess when we say, with the Apostle's Creed, "He descended to the dead." Hades, or "hell," as unhelpfully translated in some English versions of the Apostle's Creed, refers to the land of the dead. This line means that the Lord Jesus Christ, in becoming incarnate to live, die, rise, and ascend for us, experienced everything humanity in this fallen world experiences on our behalf—including the experience of his soul separating from his body and descending to the land of the dead. This "land" is "under earth," and it is one of three realms that God created (with Heaven and the Earth being the other two). Hades is the place where every soul went when they died before the time of Christ. David describes this land of the dead when he says, "If I make my bed in Sheol, you are

---

4. Martin Luther, *Luther: Letters of Spiritual Counsel*, trans. Theodore G. Tappert (Vancouver: Regent College Publications, 2003), p. 85.

5. For fuller treatments on this topic, see Matthew Y. Emerson, *He Descended to the Dead: An Evangelical Theology of Holy Saturday* (Downers Grove, IL: IVP Acaemic, 2019); Samuel D. Renihan, *Crux Mors Inferi: A Primer and Reader on the Descent of Christ* (Indeptently Published: Samuel D. Renihan, 2021).

there" (Ps. 139:8; see also Eph. 4:8-10; 1 Pet. 3:18; Phil. 2:9-11; John 5:25; Luke 16:19-31; 23:43).

Before Christ ascended, "Paradise" was located here, in Hades. Another name for this place is called "Abraham's Bosom," and it is the place Jesus promises to take the dying thief on the cross (Luke 23:43). Before the resurrection and ascension of Christ, Paradise was one of three compartments of Hades. This was the most comfortable section of Hades, with the other two ("Lower Sheol" or "the depths of the earth" and "the abyss" or "Tartarus") having been separated from it by a great chasm (see Luke 16:19-31; Job 26:6; Prov. 27:20; Rev. 9:1-2, 11; 2 Pet. 2:4). Paradise has been relocated now, however, since Christ has ascended, leading a host of captives with him (Eph. 4:8-10).

So, what happens when Jesus descends to the grave? First, he announces his victorious work on the cross to the saints in paradise, comforting them with the knowledge that his blood has atoned for their sins, and taking them with him to heaven ("he leads a hosts of captives to freedom"), and second, he announces his victory over the powers of darkness through his triumphant death on the cross, and thus "puts them to open shame" and vindicates the righteousness of God. *Now,* when people die outside of Christ, they go to Hades to experience immediate judgment (i.e., they receive the same fate as the rich man in Jesus's parable) as they await the final day of judgment when they will be thrown into the lake of fire with Satan and his demons (Rev. 20:11-15). All the souls of those who trust in him by faith, however, are brought into Paradise's new location, in his heavenly presence, where they await their resurrection and the reunion of their souls to their glorified bodies (Acts 24:15; John 5:22-29; 1 Cor. 15:12-49; 2 Cor. 5:1-10). Think about the profound comfort this is, in light of our

discussion of recapitulation in the previous chapter. Christ identifies with us at every level. He walks "through the valley of the shadow of death." To save the Old Testament saints, he had to assume a state that went as low as they went, and he *did just this!* When he blazes a trail out of the grave, he forsakes *none* of his people. I try to get at the beauty of this neglected doctrine with this poem entitled "Holy Saturday":

Lord, when they laid your body in the tomb
And your soul descended to the dead,
Did the pow'rs know you made your grave a womb—
That it was a fishhook on which you bled?
When did Sheol realize its own demise?
Its newfound captive came to liberate
Was it immediate that it despised
Its hunger for souls indiscriminate?
Did the thief imagine in your promise
He would see paradise relocated?
Abraham's bosom rose with the sunrise
When hosts of captives you liberated
Hark! Holy Saturday was death's death knell,
For on that day you snatched the keys to hell.

United to the Lamb that was Slain

Before we conclude this chapter, we ought to give our attention to one more aspect of Christ's atoning death. We might be tempted to think that Christ's substitution is an *impersonal* thing—as if this were an external transaction taking place, where God agrees to *pretend* that Christ dies in our stead. But that is not what the Scriptures portray. The imputation of our unrighteousness to Christ, and of Christ's righteousness to us—what Martin Luther called the "great exchange"—is anything but impersonal. It happens for each of us, at the experiential level, because of our *vital union* with Christ. We will have recourse to continue to consider

this doctrine in the following chapters, but for now, consider 2 Corinthians 5:21, where Paul writes, "For our sake he made him to be sin who knew no sin, so that in him we might become the righteousness of God." Let me briefly offer two observations.

Sidebar 4.3
Impeccability

The doctrine of Christ's impeccability affirms that Christ not only remained sinless throughout his life, but rather that he *could not* have sinned at all. Critics of impeccability have objected that such a construction renders Christ's temptations illegitimate or his humanity superhuman, but this misunderstands the necessity of affirming this doctrine. Christ is rendered impeccable in his incarnate life not on account of his human nature being somehow supercharged, but rather on account of the perfection of his person. Natures don't sin, persons sin in created natures. The human nature of Christ cannot be abstracted from his person—his body and soul, with its desires and wills and inclinations—are always the body and soul of the perfect Son, the second Person of the Trinity. Were he to be peccable (i.e., able to sin), we would have to affirm the possibility of a person of the Trinity being imperfect, corruptible, and sinful.

First, notice the severity of *sin*. Paul says, "*for our sake* God made Christ to be sin." The second person of the Trinity, the eternal Son of God, assumed a human nature to himself, and lived and breathed on this planet. And he, this God-man, the Father made to be sin *for our sake*? Why? Why does he do this *for our sake*? What does it benefit us for him to be made sin? The answer, as uncomfortably as it may sit with us, is that sin is who we are apart from him. Christ was made our sin. The only way that we could benefit from any sort of exchange with God was for the Son of God to be made the embodiment of sin. That's how wretched we were. That's how dreadful our situation was. Our identity was bound to sin;

our fundamental disposition was in opposition to God. You could put it like this: the reason that Jesus endured the full crushing weight of the wrath of God on the cross is because, when he was on the cross, he looked like you and me in our sinful condition apart from him.

Second, notice how union with Christ makes imputation possible. The active and passive obedience of Christ imputed to us in salvation are not benefits that can be abstracted from Christ himself. We receive these things through our union with him. You see, my union with Christ means that the Holy Spirit has connected me to—and incorporated me into—Christ, such that his life becomes mine, his death becomes mine, and his resurrection becomes mine. For me to be united to Christ means that it would now be unjust for God to sentence me to eternal death on account of my sin, because, in Christ, *I have already been put to death for those sins!* In Christ, my record of debt that stood against me with its legal demands has already been nailed to the cross and buried in the grave. In Christ, I have been resurrected to walk in newness of life, free from the condemnation that drove me to be crucified with him. Union with Christ is how his passive obedience is something we can benefit from. In his union with us, Christ steps into our sinful shoes (without himself sinning or properly being called *fallen*),[6] he walks the mile in those shoes to the cross. When all is said and done, we can rest assured that God is not "letting us off the hook" for a single sin we commit. We are sentenced to death for every one of them, but we are sentenced to death for every one of them *in Christ*. Behold, friends, the beauty of this God-man's sacrificial death. See how it is the turning point in the Trinity's plan of salvation and let yourself be dumbstruck by its loveliness. Where else could we find

---

6. See chapter 3, and sidebar 4.2.

such beauty and grace? Where else could we find such awe-inspiring mercy? Jonathan Edwards captures the beauty in the ugly cross powerfully:

> It is by seeing the excellency of Christ's Person that the saints are made sensible of the preciousness of His blood, and its sufficiency to atone for sin; for therein consists the preciousness of Christ's blood, that it is the blood of so excellent and amiable a Person .... By this sight of the moral beauty of divine things is seen the beauty of the way of salvation by Christ; for that consists in the beauty of the moral perfections of God, which wonderfully shines forth in every step of this method of salvation from beginning to end.[7]

* * *

Our Great God, we are humbled by your Word. When we read who we are apart from the grace of Christ, we are brought to our knees. "Still weak," and "ungodly"—these words pierce our hearts. Before you came, Lord Jesus, we were not righteous; we were not good. In no way is anyone's death for ours fitting— let alone your death, precious Jesus. "Still sinners"—words like an anchor tied to our necks; we droop in your arms. We were sinners. We were unrighteous. Our hearts were jet black with sin. We were unable to utter anything but bile—this we know with not the slightest doubt, for we still walk around with the same skin and bone. The same sin allures. The same bile dribbles out of our lips. The old crucified man stubbornly tries to mimic resurrection. Oh! Our sin! Yes, Lord, while you show us a little of the depth of our sin, you do not let us despair. By contrast, you remind us of the depth of your grace. We have not been saved from little. We have been saved from much. We have not even seen the bottom of the chasm of our sin, yet "where

---

7. Jonathan Edwards, *Works of Jonathan Edwards*, 2:274–75.

sin increased, grace abounded all the more (Rom 5:20)." Father, thank you for making your Son, who knew no sin, become sin for our sake, so that in him we might become the righteousness of God. Dear Jesus, thank you for obeying the Father for us, in your living and dying, in your suffering and obedience, that we might be reconciled to you. Holy Spirit, thank you for uniting us to Christ in his life, death, and resurrection. Triune God, thank you for reconciling yourself to us, and entrusting us with the ministry of reconciliation. Amen.

5

The Resurrection

Christic, the Cosmic Firstfruits

The word "catastrophe," especially when referring to literature, carries the idea of a sudden and unexpected disaster in the narrative. A drastic drop off in the story. The catastrophe is an all-too-common experience, not just in literature, but in our own lives. Sudden and unexpected death in the family. A medical diagnosis that makes your stomach drop. The discovery of betrayal from someone you love and trust. All catastrophes.

We are well acquainted with the "catastrophe." But J.R.R. Tolkien coined an antonym for catastrophe: the *eucatastrophe*. This is the sudden and unexpected turn of sorrowful tides; the punctuated uptick in the storyline that begins the happy-ever-after. Without expectation, everything begins to go *well* just at the point we were expecting for everything to end in tragedy. In Tolkien's *Lord of the Rings* novels, there are several eucatastrophe moments, but my favorite is the one he writes for his character, Sam. After masterfully articulating catastrophe after catastrophe over the scope of three novels, Tolkien has left the reader ready to curl up in a ball and hide forever. The fact that you may know how the story ends does

little to alleviate this impulse. I have read these novels several times, and yet without fail, the feeling I experience of despair as Frodo and Sam lay on the side of Mount Doom, settling in to die next to one another, is nearly overwhelming. And then it happens. Sam gets his eucatastrophe. He wakes up and is greeted by Gandalf—his friend and sage, who died in front of him two novels back in one of Tolkien's most tragic catastrophes—and he informs Sam that "a great shadow has passed," with a laugh that sounded like "music, or like water in a parched land." Sam's eucatastrophe is epitomized by the question that bubbles up within him from sheer bewildered ecstasy and joy: "Is everything sad going to come untrue?"[1] Now *that* is a great question. And only one event in human history gives us any reason to hope for an affirmative answer: the resurrection of Jesus Christ.

In this chapter, I want to revel in the sunrise of Jesus's resurrection—the great eucatastrophic moment in the storyline of God's salvation history. "Long lay the world in sin and error pining, till he *appeared*," we sing at Christmas. And yet, Christmas cannot be separated from Paschal Sunday (or, if you like, Easter). All the brightness of Christ's incarnate life hinges on the presence or absence of this eucatastrophe. Without it, the story of Jesus is a tragedy. The resurrection is *the* single event that turns the tragedy of Christ's life story into a glorious comedy.

For our primary point of departure, we'll use the account of the resurrection in John's Gospel, considering this episode in three scenes.

---

1. J.R.R. Tolkein, *The Lord of the Rings: The Return of the King* (New York: Delray, 1994), p. 246.

Scene I: The Disciples at the Tomb

Now on the first day of the week Mary Magdalene came to the tomb early, while it was still dark, and saw that the stone had been taken away from the tomb. So she ran and went to Simon Peter and the other disciple, the one whom Jesus loved, and said to them, "They have taken the Lord out of the tomb, and we do not know where they have laid him." So Peter went out with the other disciple, and they were going toward the tomb. Both of them were running together, but the other disciple outran Peter and reached the tomb first. And stooping to look in, he saw the linen cloths lying there, but he did not go in. Then Simon Peter came, following him, and went into the tomb. He saw the linen cloths lying there, and the face cloth, which had been on Jesus' head, not lying with the linen cloths but folded up in a place by itself. Then the other disciple, who had reached the tomb first, also went in, and he saw and believed; for as yet they did not understand the Scripture, that he must rise from the dead. Then the disciples went back to their homes (John 20:1-10).

John shares his testimony in this passage. He was the first disciple who believed in the resurrection, when he "saw and believed." This is where all the pieces snap into place for John. He sees the empty tomb and the linens, and all Jesus's formerly obscure dark sayings about "raising this temple" become clear (John 2:19-21). He believes.

As we read the description of the linens, how can we not contrast this episode with John 11:44 and the raising of Lazarus? "The man who had died came out, his hands and feet bound with linen strips, and his face wrapped with a cloth." In *this* scene at the end of John's Gospel, those grave clothes don't cling to Jesus the way they did with Lazarus—they are lying neatly where Jesus had previously laid. Evidently, there is something altogether different about Jesus' resurrection. At the raising of Lazarus, Jesus demonstrates his authority

over death. But the man he raises from the dead is still dead in his trespasses and will die again. He still has his funeral garments. Not so with Jesus' resurrection.

John continues in his account:

> But Mary stood weeping outside the tomb, and as she wept she stooped to look into the tomb. And she saw two angels in white, sitting where the body of Jesus had lain, one at the head and one at the feet. They said to her, "Woman, why are you weeping?" She said to them, "They have taken away my Lord, and I do not know where they have laid him." Having said this, she turned around and saw Jesus standing, but she did not know that it was Jesus. Jesus said to her, "Woman, why are you weeping? Whom are you seeking?" Supposing him to be the gardener, she said to him, "Sir, if you have carried him away, tell me where you have laid him, and I will take him away." (John 20:11-15).

Mary hasn't come to understand what John has realized at this point, so she is still grieving. But her sadness is *beautiful*. You get an idea of how overwhelmed she was with sorrow by the fact that she's greeted by two angels who ask her why she's crying, and she simply says, "They have taken away my Lord, and I do not know where they have laid him." Such a response doesn't ordinarily spring up from people who meet angelic beings in the Scriptures; they typically cower in fear. But Mary is so overcome with sadness that she lacks the awareness of what's happening. Such a picture of the devotion she had for Jesus. The body of her Lord is gone, and she doesn't know where it is. First his death: catastrophe. Now his body is missing: catastrophe.

And then, Mary gets her eucatastrophe.

"Jesus said to her, 'Mary.' She turned and said to him in Aramaic, 'Rabboni!' (which means Teacher)" (John 20:16). He says *her name*. "I know that voice," she says to herself. With only the one word, the sound of his voice was like "music,"

or "water in a parched land." As the sound of his voice sunk into her ear, the light of his presence instantly flooded the darkness of that moment of despair and isolation, and Mary experienced the ecstasy of being shot through the heart with sudden joy. I doubt her weeping stopped. I suspect it tripled in intensity. "My sheep hear my voice, I know my own and my own know me," Jesus had said (John 10:1-21), and here we see this intimate dynamic unfold. A lost and worried and despairing sheep hears the familiar voice of her shepherd, and she responds.

It also should not surprise us that Jesus is mistaken for a "gardener" in this passage. In one sense, that is *exactly* what he is; he is the Second Adam, who undoes *in a garden* all the tragedy set into motion by the first Adam, who brought about the curse of sin *in a garden*. Adam was a gardener-priest, who, rather than working the garden and bearing the fruit of life for the sake of ordered praise and worship as he had been commanded, ushered in the tomb of death and decay. And now, here stands Christ, the final gardener-priest, standing in *another* garden with *another* woman, having defeated death and springing out of the tomb as the first-fruits of the New Creation. [2] He is making the sad things come untrue.

Isn't our Second Adam glorious? Isn't our Good Shepherd *lovely*? He orchestrated this moment for Mary. This all-knowing, omniscient Son of God knew Mary was there with Peter and John. He knew that Peter and John would leave. And he knew that Mary would stay, frozen in grief. Doubtless he saw all three there at the tomb from a distance, and *he waited until he was alone with Mary*. He had prepared

---

2. For more on this idea of Adam as *priest*, and Eden as a garden-temple, see J.V. Fesko, *Last Things First: Unlocking Genesis 1-3 with the Christ of Eschatology* (Ross-Shire, UK: Mentor, 2007), ch. 2.

this moment—this the first of his resurrection encounters—for *her*. He had prepared a *eucatastrophe* just for Mary.

Jesus must tell her, "Do not cling to me," because she surely lunged toward him to (as my son would say when he was a toddler) *"squeeze the stuffing out of him."* Now, some throughout Church history have speculated that Jesus's command not to cling to him was a rebuke for unseemly behavior. I strongly disagree with this interpretation. Self-debasing, wholehearted devotion to Christ is never scorned by him. Go back and look at Mary the sister of Lazarus in John 12:1-8 for proof. No, Jesus loves that kind of overwhelming affection. Rather, he tells her not to cling to him because it's not time to cling to him *yet*. He makes this reason explicit, when he says, "for I have not yet ascended to the Father." It's as if he's saying, "I know Mary, I know, you want to embrace me and never let go. But I'm not completely finished with what I came here to do. *I'm so close!* The tide has been turned. Death has been dealt the death blow. But soon I'll need to ascend to the Father to fulfill all the promises I've made to you. So go tell the others that the beginning of the end is here."

He says, "go to *my* brothers,"—as if to reiterate that, despite what his scattered sheep may be worrying about considering their abandonment of him (Matt. 26:56; John 19:25-27), *he still loves them*. He tells her to announce, "I am ascending to my Father and your Father, to my God and your God" (John 20:17) Oh, what a glorious phrase! With several words, Jesus announces their familial relation to his God. He, the eternal Son, has in his life, death, and resurrection, made them sons as well. The Father he has for all eternity called "Father" is now, in him, *their Father too*. What he is by nature he has now made them by grace.

And with a swift obedience, Mary does what Christ commanded (John 20:18).

Scene II: Jesus Commissioning His Disciples

> On the evening of that day, the first day of the week, the doors being locked where the disciples were for fear of the Jews, Jesus came and stood among them and said to them, "Peace be with you." When he had said this, he showed them his hands and his side. Then the disciples were glad when they saw the Lord. Jesus said to them again, "Peace be with you. As the Father has sent me, even so I am sending you." And when he had said this, he breathed on them and said to them, "Receive the Holy Spirit. If you forgive the sins of any, they are forgiven them; if you withhold forgiveness from any, it is withheld." (John 20:19-23).

Now, setting aside the curious nature of his resurrected body (which, by the way, walks through walls not because he is more ethereal than them, but rather because matter in the fallen and sinful world is more phantasmal than *his* glorious body!), notice the tight connection here between (a) the "peace" of Jesus, (b) the mission of the disciples, (c) their reception of the Holy Spirit, and (d) the authority to pronounce the forgiveness of sins. All these concepts hold together.

"Peace" he says, to his troubled and conflicted disciples. "Peace" he says to these men who had abandoned him— who scattered when he was struck. "Peace" he says to his worried friends, who just saw him crucified and are now surely wondering what's next on the agenda of his enemies. "Peace," says he who alone in the history of humankind went toe to toe with Death and came out on the other side with his opponent under his bootheel.

And what does it look like to give "peace" in this episode? It looks like giving his disciples *himself*, in the presence of the Holy Spirit, who empowers them to live on his mission and proclaim the gospel—the message that offers forgiveness of sin. He had told them before the crucifixion, "I will not leave you as orphans; I will come to you" (John 14:18), and this promise fits squarely within the context of Christ's description of the Spirit's future ministry and arrival. The Father's love will be manifested in this way: Christ and the Father will "make their home" with the disciples, and this will occur when the Spirit arrives (John 14:23-30).

With this context in view, Christ "breathes" on his disciples and says, "receive the Holy Spirit" (John 20:22; 14:26-27). This demonstrates, in part, that he has the prerogative—along with the Father—to send the Holy Spirit to them. We should not assume that such a prerogative bespeaks a hierarchy of authority within the inner life of the Trinity, with the Spirit on the bottom rung of the latter. The Father and the Son sending the Spirit in the economy of redemption rather bespeaks the eternal relation of the Spirit's *procession* from the Father and the Son. In the same way that the Son's eternal generation makes *his* incarnation (rather than the Father's or the Spirit's) *fitting*, so too the Spirit's eternal procession from the Father and Son makes his being sent (and breathed) by the Father and Son fitting as well (see John 14:16, 26; 16:7).

But does this "breathing" mean that the disciples, in this moment, receive the Holy Spirit in an indwelling fashion— the way he promised in previous chapters? The answer has to be no, for a couple of important reasons. First, throughout chapters 13–17, Jesus has linked *that kind of* arrival of the Holy Spirit with his *ascension* to the Father. The Holy Spirit *can't* come until he completes his work and ascends into

heaven first. Jesus has been very clear about that point (John 16:7). But second, notice how Jesus associates their reception of the Holy Spirit with (a) their being sent out on mission, and (b) the forgiveness of sins. We don't see those things happen in dramatic fashion until we turn the pages of our Bibles over to Acts chapter 2, when the disciples receive the Holy Spirit on the day of Pentecost, and Peter stands up and proclaims the gospel, resulting in the salvation of 3,000 people—i.e., 3,000 people have their *sins forgiven* (Acts 2:1-41). So, this episode in John's Gospel is a kind of parable of what will happen some fifty days from now when Jesus has ascended to the Father. Jesus is telling his disciples what they can expect, and what he intends to do through them: the mission he was sent by the Father and anointed to perform is further extended and proclaimed by his blood-bought, Spirit-anointed people.

The disciples, here, are given their marching orders ("I am sending you"), their authoritative prerogative ("forgive sins"), and are instructed as to where the power to accomplish these things will come from ("receive the Holy Spirit"). In this way, this passage is John's version of "the Great Commission" (Matt. 28:18-20) and his description of the Church's use of the "keys to the Kingdom" (Matt. 16:16-20, 18:15-20). *There* the language is "whatever you bind on earth will have been bound in heaven, and whatever you loosen on earth will have been loosed in heaven," but here it's "If you forgive the sins of any, they are forgiven them; if you withhold forgiveness from any, it is withheld." In both passages, the idea is the same: the disciples of Christ are those who pronounce the forgiveness of sins. They alone bear the message that grants forgiveness.

All this is why Christians can say to a lost and dying world, with all the authority of God's Word, "If you trust in the life, death, resurrection and ascension of Jesus Christ for

your salvation, your sins are forgiven, but if you don't, they aren't." Our authority, as disciples of Jesus Christ, is one of pronouncing what *is* the case. Jesus here does not imply that the disciples can arbitrarily decide whose sins are forgiven and whose aren't. God alone grants forgiveness. But we can say that anyone who truly trusts in the message of Christ's Church *is* forgiven, and anyone who doesn't, isn't.

Having documented the resurrected Christ's marching orders, John takes us straight into the third scene for our consideration.

Scene III: Jesus Gently Rebuking Unbelief

> Now Thomas, one of the twelve, called the Twin, was not with them when Jesus came. So the other disciples told him, "We have seen the Lord." But he said to them, "Unless I see in his hands the mark of the nails, and place my finger into the mark of the nails, and place my hand into his side, I will never believe."
>
> Eight days later, his disciples were inside again, and Thomas was with them. Although the doors were locked, Jesus came and stood among them and said, "Peace be with you." Then he said to Thomas, "Put your finger here, and see my hands; and put out your hand, and place it in my side. Do not disbelieve, but believe." Thomas answered him, "My Lord and my God!" Jesus said to him, "Have you believed because you have seen me? Blessed are those who have not seen and yet have believed." (John 20:24-27)

This word from Jesus is desperately needed today. Here we see Thomas, the "realist." The one who's simply "wired to be skeptical," he might have said. And yet, without burdening Thomas with a crushing demand to have absolute unyielding and perfect faith, Christ does not commend him for his skepticism. What John describes for us with these stark words, "Do not disbelieve, but believe," is a rebuke. Such

a rebuke, though incredibly gentle and accommodating (a point made clear by the fact that Jesus invites Thomas to erase any lingering doubt by touching his side and hands), is not likely to be received well in our own age. Out of an effort to be authentic and transparent, we have all but turned doubt into a virtue, as if the only credible testimony of faith in Christ is the one that is hard-won through deep angst and doubt. Though few would say so, in some circles it almost appears as though *assurance* isn't even something desirable, since ongoing doubt is the sure mark of authenticity. But we must take our cues from Scripture in the way we describe our experiences. And while doubt may not be described in every instance as a vice, it is *never* portrayed as a *virtue*. Doubt is rather a mark of corruption at some level. It clearly communicates a lack of wholeness. This is not to say that the Lord may not have good purposes for sovereignly allowing us to experience these kinds of seasons. Such seasons are what Christians throughout the history of the Church have called "the dark night of the soul," and it is not uncommon for these tragic periods to yield some of the most enriching and delightful epiphanies about God's goodness. But the throbbing ache to *exit* this dark night is a sure sign that someone is experiencing it as God intends: God does not want us to settle in a state of indecision, let alone a state of expressing deep suspicion towards his promises.

Of course, profound delicacy is required here. For one thing, not all doubt is created equal. As we see here, there is a big difference between sorrowful Mary Magdalene, who struggles to put the pieces together, and Doubting Thomas, who announces his skepticism with flamboyance. Also, as I never tire of saying, churches ought to strive to create the kind of environments where sins and struggles and doubts and fears are shared freely, without the fear of shame or

condemnation from one another. God forbid we ever *gasp* in horrified shock or disgust in response to humble and contrite confession. We should strive to be *unshockable* listeners of confession—brimming with the readiness to apply the balm of the gospel to wounded consciences. But the freedom to confess sins and struggles does not equate to the celebration of sins and struggles.

The problem is not how *frequently* we talk about doubt. If you struggle with doubt, you *should* talk about it *often*. The question is, *how do you talk about your doubt?* Is it a badge of honor? Is doubt the demonstration of your credibility among unbelievers, proof that you are a truly "open-minded" Christian? Or is it a tragedy to lament, and a trial to overcome? Do you point it out to your fellow believers to show how much of a free-thinker you are, or do you point it out as a cry for help to come to a place of resting in God's promises? Do you coddle your doubt or do you seek by God's help to overcome it?

In our text in John 20, Thomas chooses rightly. He goes from being a haughty skeptic to being Christ-worshiper through *one* interaction with the beautiful man, Christ Jesus. This is what Christ accomplishes with his gracious approach to Thomas: transformation. The starkness could not be more profound. No one in John's Gospel pronounces doubt quite as emphatically as Thomas ("… I will *never* believe"), and no one in John's gospel pronounces such high Christology as quite as emphatically or explicitly as Thomas either ("My Lord and my God!"). Thomas had encountered the most beautiful man to ever live, and it shows.

So much for John's account of the history's archetypical eucatastrophe. Now, I'd like to consider the resurrection of Christ in light of theology. What I wish to show below is that Christian theology isn't *Christian* without the resurrection

of Jesus. Therefore, coming to grips with the beauty of his defeat over the grave is essential for us to truly grasp the beauty of the rest of his person and work. The doctrines of our salvation need the resurrection to really *sing*.

The Resurrection and Our Salvation

In Chapter 3, we considered the "tale of two Adams," as portrayed by Romans 5, where Paul tells of how "sin came into the world through one man, and death through sin, and so death spread to all men because all sinned" (Rom. 5:12). The work of Christ in the incarnation, we saw, was a work of *recapitulation*. All of humanity has been plunged into the muck and mire of death in Adam. To wade through this thick sludge and climb out on the other side is impossible. Humanity is stuck; enclosed and swallowed whole by death. This is what the sin of Adam brought: he dragged humanity into the throws of death.

But in the gospel, the Second Adam plunged headlong into this miry pit. He plunged so deep into death, in fact, that for three days the surface lay still, undisturbed, quietly boasting in victory. But then, on the first Easter morning, for the first time in human history (but not the last) the surface of death's gate broke. Jesus, the Second Adam, blasted out of death's clutches, carrying with him a new humanity—the spoils of victory. On that Easter morning, Jesus stepped on Death's face as he stormed out of the tomb carrying with him his posterity. I love how John Milton describes this victory over death, foretold by the Son, in his epic poem, *Paradise Lost*:

> But I shall rise victorious, and subdue
> My vanquisher, spoiled of his vaunted spoil;
> Death his death's wound shall then receive, and stoop
> Inglorious, of his mortal sting disarmed.

I through the ample air in triumph high
Shall lead Hell captive maugre Hell, and show
The powers of darkness bound. Thou at the sight
Pleased, out of Heaven long absent, and return,
Father, to see thy face, wherein no cloud
Of anger shall remain, but peace assured,
And reconcilement; wrath shall be no more
Thenceforth, but in thy presence joy entire.[3]

Without the resurrection of Jesus, his story is simply another example of death swallowing up another mortal, and we have no hope that "all the sad things will come untrue." There is no assurance of promises kept without the resurrection. Apart from this eucatastrophe, there is no new lineage into which we might be grafted. We are born in Adam, and the end of his family line is the grave. But we who are born again in Christ are part of a family line that comes up out of the grave.

Additionally, the resurrection makes sense of our doctrine of justification. It is no throwaway line for Paul to say that Christ was "delivered up for our trespasses and raised for our justification" (Rom. 4:25). In his death, Jesus offers up a sacrifice to God on our behalf. He himself

---

3. John Milton, *Paradise Lost*, ed. John Leonard (New York, NY: Penguin Books, 2003), p. 59. In quoting Milton, I do feel some obligation to mention that in 1823, an anonymous and unpublished book was found and later attributed to him, called *De Doctrina*, which is something of a heretical, non-trinitarian systematic theology. For nearly the entirety of his career, Milton was blind and had to dictate his books to his secretary, and this document was discovered to be written by his secretary's hand. While most scholarship affirms that this document is Milton's, there are some scholars who object. I remain unconvinced that we should attribute the document to Milton, and I definitely don't think his *Paradise Lost* should be read through the lens of *De Doctrina*. *Paradise Lost* has some portions that are only questionable if the poetic imagery is stretched too far. In general, it is a richly Christian and deeply edifying poem, which is why I'm comfortable with quoting it.

is the sacrifice, as we saw in the previous chapter. Christ is the pure sacrifice, who was faithful where Adam and Israel and you and I are unfaithful (i.e., he is actively and passively obedient). That's his offering: his perfect obedience in life and death. And he takes that offering of himself and lays it up on the cross-shaped altar, and says, "This is my body, broken for my people. This is my blood, shed for my people."

And then he dies.

And for three days, the cosmos holds its breath. Will this offering be acceptable? Will this death satisfy the wrath owed? Will this righteous life grant eternal peace to others?

And in the resurrection, God says, absolutely, and emphatically, "Yes!" He says, "I gladly accept this sacrificial offering. All who are by faith found in my beloved Son, have the righteous requirements of the law satisfied, the penalty for sin paid, and are accounted as not guilty and are now declared righteous!" This is what it means to be justified, and without the resurrection, it doesn't exist. Without the resurrection, the cross of Christ is at worst just another example of Roman execution and is at best an uncertainty. Without the resurrection, we have no hope that our sins are actually forgiven on account of the death of Christ; we have nothing to assure us that his sacrifice on our behalf is acceptable. "And if Christ has not been raised," says Paul in 1 Corinthians 15:18, "your faith is futile and you are still in your sins." But in the resurrection, God the Father has shouted a word of assurance, and his voice echoes throughout all human history: "Justification is surely, objectively, definitively offered in this God-man, Jesus Christ." One of the fruits that flows from the assurance of justification—guaranteed by the resurrection—is the gift of a cleansed conscience. Think about the consolation of the forgiveness of sins we have through the resurrection. Who

does not desperately need such a consolation? No age or culture escapes the need for assuaging the guilty conscience.

Shakespeare, Guilt, and the Assurance of Resurrection

I love how William Shakespeare portrayed this deeply human experience of a tormented conscience in his various plays.

> Methought I heard a voice cry "Sleep no more!
> Macbeth does murder sleep" – the innocent sleep,
> Sleep that knits up the raveled sleave of care,
> The death of each day's life, sore labor's bath,
> Balm of hurt minds, great nature's second course,
> Chief nourisher in life's feast.[4]

These are the words of Shakespeare's character, Macbeth, the night he sealed his fate. The story of this play is simple and straightforward enough: Macbeth, the Thane of Glamis and noble servant of Duncan, King of Scotland, gets a taste for ambition and power and seeks after it headlong, to his own destruction and the destruction of many others. At the first promise of glory and power, Macbeth experiences the awakening of a thirst that refuses to be satiated.

Macbeth is enticed at the beginning of this play by three sister witches, who foretell two incredible predictions: first, he will be raised up from Thane of Glamis to Thane of Cawdor, and second, from Thane of Cawdor to King of Scotland. The first prediction comes true apart from any action taken on Macbeth's part, to his great surprise, when he is greeted as Thane of Cawdor ("The Thane of Cawdor lives. Why do you dress me in borrowed robes?").[5] He discovers at this point that the previous Thane of Cawdor was a traitor and was

---

4. William Shakespeare, *Macbeth*, ed. Stephen Orgel (New York, NY: Penguin Books, 2016), Act II.2.
5. Shakespeare, *Macbeth*, Act I.3.

to therefore be executed. It is at *this* point in the story that Macbeth is faced with a decision. With the first prediction foretold by the three witches now come true, would he trust the other to fortune as well, or would he tempt fate and take matters into his own hand? At this point in the story, Macbeth is not so corrupt as he would become, and he totters.

Lady Macbeth, however, makes up for all the resolution her husband lacks: "Glamis thou art, and Cawdor, and shalt be What thou art promised," she says to herself, speaking of her husband, "Yet do I fear thy nature. It is too full o' th' milk of human kindness To catch the nearest way. Art not without ambition, but without The illness should attend it."[6] Lady Macbeth fears her husband's failure of nerve. She regrets his lack of "illness," an illness to do what is necessary. She *wants* for the ambition within him to grow ever more insatiable. And so, she calls on dark spirits to help direct her husband to the destiny of his greatness:

> … Come, you spirits
> That tend on mortal thoughts, unsex me here,
> And fill me from the crown to the tow topfull
> Of direst cruelty. Make thick my blood;
> Stop up th' access and passage to remorse,
> That no compunctious visitings of nature
> Shake my fell purpose nor keep peace between
> Th' effect and it. Come to my woman's breasts
> And take my milk for gall, you murd'ring ministers,
> Wherever in your sightless substances
> You wait on nature's mischief.[7]

Lady Macbeth prays for the resolve to influence her husband to take matters into his own hands. She prays for the resolve

---

6. Shakespeare, *Macbeth*, Act I.5.
7. Shakespeare, *Macbeth*, Act I.5.

to pressure Macbeth to murder Duncan. And it would seem that this twisted "prayer" is answered, for soon after, when Duncan sleeps as a guest in Macbeth's home, and Macbeth wavers in their murderous plan once again, Lady Macbeth conjures up all the dark nerve she begged the spirits for. Shaming Macbeth for his "unmanly" decision to spare the innocent Duncan, Lady Macbeth, having "unsexed herself," abandons her maternal instincts and goes horribly dark in her commitment to shock her husband into action:

> … I have given suck, and know
> How tender 'tis to love the babe that milks me:
> I would, while it was smiling in my face,
> Have plucked my nipple from his boneless gums
> And dashed the brains out, had I so sworn as you
> Have done to this.[8]

She succeeds in putting confidence back in her husband to stop at nothing to gain his ambitious goal to be king (a goal, we should remind ourselves, which was absolutely *foreign* to Macbeth's mind at the beginning of the play, but which now consumes his imaginations). Up until this point, no concrete step had been taken. Macbeth is tormented, in a way, by the thought of not becoming king. But after he commits murder, and the blood of Duncan first stains his hands (and then his wife's hands as well, when she plants Macbeth's bloody knives on Duncan's sleeping guards), he is tormented in quite another way. When Macbeth murdered Duncan, he murdered his own *sleep*. "Methought I heard a voice cry 'Sleep no more! Macbeth does murder sleep' – the innocent sleep."[9]

There is no rest, there is no relief, there is no safety for Macbeth, though he gains unimaginable power and

---

8. Shakespeare, *Macbeth,* Act I.7.
9. Shakespeare, *Macbeth*, Act II.2.

greatness. To maintain this power and greatness, he sinks further and further into the mire of sin. Whereas contemplation of murdering Duncan left him reeling with indecision toward the beginning of the play, by its end he is frantic to maintain control: willing to murder his best friend, women, and children to hold onto his position. And in all this, Macbeth is sleepless:

> But let the frame of things disjoint, both the worlds suffer,
> Ere we will eat our meal in fear, and sleep
> In the affliction of these terrible dreams
> That shake us nightly. Better be with the dead,
> Whom we, to gain our peace, have sent to peace,
> Than on the torture of the mind to lie
> In restless ecstasy. Duncan is in his grave;
> After life's fitful fever he sleeps well.
> Treason has done his worst: nor steel nor poison,
> Malice domestic, foreign levy, nothing,
> Can touch him further.[10]

Macbeth, having sent Duncan to peace (i.e., the grave) in order to gain his own peace (i.e., the position of kingship), has given Duncan true rest, in exchange for an "ecstasy" that turned out to be "restless" and "torture of the mind." This brittle, paranoid fear reveals Macbeth's guilty conscience, while complete mental breakdown and vivid nightmares reveals Lady Macbeth's:

> Out, damned spot! Out, I say! One – two – why then 'tis time to do't. Hell is murky. Fie, my lord, fie! a soldier and afeard? What need we fear who knows it, when none can call our power to account? Yet who would have thought the old man to have so much blood in him?... Here's the smell of the blood still. All the perfumes of Arabia will not sweeten this little hand. Oh, oh, oh![11]

---

10. Shakespeare, *Macbeth,* Act III.2.
11. Shakespeare, *Macbeth,* Act V.1.

Is this not the sound a self-accused conscience makes? "Oh!" Indulge me with another powerful Shakespearian example of a guilty conscience. We find this example in Claudius's fitful monologue in the tragedy, *Hamlet*. Claudius is Hamlet's uncle, and he was made King of Denmark after conspiring against and murdering Hamlet's father—the rightful King. In one scene, Claudius is struck with the shame of his guilt and says this:

> O, my offense is rank, it smells to heaven;
> It hath the primal eldest curse upon't,
> A brother's murder. Pray can I not,
> Though inclination be as sharp as will.
> My stronger guilt defeats my strong intent,
> And like a man to double business bound
> I stand in pause where I shall first begin,
> And both neglect. What if this cursed hand
> Were thicker than itself with brother's blood,
> Is there not rain enough in the sweet heavens
> To wash it white as snow?[12]

Claudius could not bring himself to pray because of the shame of guilt. He had committed the "primal eldest curse," the same sin as Cain—the murder of a brother. And he asks, "What if this cursed hand Were thicker than itself with brother's blood?" In other words, "What if there is more of my brother's blood on my hand than there is my own flesh and bone?" In that case, is it even likely that heaven has enough rain to wash the guilt away? Have you ever felt paralyzed by the guilt of your sin like this? Have you ever been paralyzed by shame? What's the cure?" Well I can tell you most assuredly that the cure is not a look *inward*—you

---

12. William Shakespeare, *Hamlet: The Tragical History of Hamlet Prince of Denmark*, ed. A. R. Braunmuller (New York, NY: Penguin Books, 2016), Act III.3.

keep looking inward and you will only find more reasons for more shame.

The cure for this kind of paralyzing shame is not to search for how precious you are, it is to behold how precious Christ is, and what an unfathomable grace he has shown to bring about your reconciliation. The cure for this kind of shame is to be reminded that Christ was not compelled to lay his life down for you by your beauty—you had none. It is not our intrinsic worth that is seen in the gospel—as if God simply could not be happy until we were restored to him in salvation. No, it works the other way around. It's not that Christ was compelled to pay such a price because we were so worthy, but rather, we are now made worthy *because of the infinite price he paid to purchase us.* And here's the point we must not forget: without the resurrection, there is no assurance that his offering is sufficient to pay for our redemption and cleanse our consciences. Without the resurrection, we have no reason to feel anything but pensive worry about our sin— we are Macbeth, Lady Macbeth, and Claudius, haunted by a tortured conscience with no hope of relief. But if we trust by faith in the resurrected Lord Jesus, we are assured by the empty tomb he "borrowed" that forgiveness of sins is guaranteed in him.

This is what our new status as justified means for us: reconciliation (Rom. 5:1-11, 2 Cor. 5:11-21). The sin that stood between us and God has been removed. Every reason for enmity between us and God has been undermined—we now have peace, and the resurrection assures this.

To use a biblical illustration, recall Luke's account of the crucifixion, when he tells us that "the curtain of the temple was torn in two" when Christ died (Luke 23:44-46). This was the curtain that separated the holy presence of God from the unholy presence of man. And Jesus's death *tears*

it down. This is truly an amazing thing! But let me ask this question: who among us would dare to walk through it if Jesus is not our forerunner? Would anyone of us volunteer to walk into the holy of holies simply because the veil is torn? Would we not all be like John at the tomb, timidly peeking in (John 20:5)? But in the resurrection, Jesus takes us by the hand and, with a quick and determined pace, walks us into the throne room of grace, and places our hand in God the Father's, who looks down at us with eyes full of acceptance (consider Heb. 10:19-22).

All these truths and more are ours because of our union to the *resurrected* Christ. Speaking of union, could you imagine how hopeless of a doctrine union with Christ would be if he remained in the tomb? Just think how the Systematic Theology textbooks would read: "In the doctrine of union with Christ, the Holy Spirit mysteriously unites you to a man who dies for sin … Next doctrine …" And we would all be left thinking, "Do I really need that? Do I need to be united to a man who dies in the penalty of sin? Won't I do that all on my own when I die?" But once we throw the resurrection into the doctrine of union with Christ, it begins to sing. The song resounds thusly, "The Spirit of God has united you to Christ, such that his righteous life becomes your righteous life, and in his death, you die for your sins, and in his burial, you are buried in the grave with all your sins, but in his resurrection, you are resurrected with him, leaving your sin and the condemnation thereof to rot six feet under" (see Rom. 6:1-14)!

Earlier, I quoted from the Son's speech in Milton's *Paradise Lost*, wherein he determined to accomplish the atoning work of redemption for mankind. After that speech, Milton portrays the Father's response, in which he commands the

heavenly angels to glorify the Son. In his speech, the Father assures,

> … so in thee
> As from a second root shall be restored,
> As many as are restored, without thee none.
> His crime makes guilty all his sons; thy merit
> Imputed shall absolve them who renounce
> Their own both righteous and unrighteous deeds,
> And live in thee transplanted, and from thee
> Receive new life.[13]

The restoration the Father speaks of in Milton's poetic portrayal is what theologians call the Covenant of Redemption (i.e., the trinitarian pact to determine to save mankind through the gospel before the foundations of the earth), which is only possible because of the resurrection. [14] The merit of Christ, he says, will be imputed only to those who "renounce their own both righteous and unrighteous deeds." That is, only those who refuse to attempt to win their own justification ("righteous deeds") and who repent of sin to trust in Christ ("unrighteous deeds") will receive the imputation of Christ's merit. These people are those who will "live in [Christ] transplanted, and from [him] receive new life." What good would it do to be transplanted into a dead man (even if he lived perfectly before ending up in the grave)? Because Christ is the risen and resurrected Lord, being transplanted into him is the means of receiving new life.

And, as we'll see in the following chapter, Christ's resurrection not only impacts our Christian life now, it

---

13. Milton, *Paradise Lost*, p. 60.

14. For a fuller description of this covenant, see J. V. Fesko, *The Trinity and the Covenant of Redemption* (Ross-Shire, UK: Christian Focus, 2016).

guarantees our own resurrection in the life to come. Recall Jesus's conversation with Martha in John chapter 11 after Lazarus died. To console her, Jesus says to Martha, "Lazarus will live again." "Yeah Jesus," Martha replies, "I know he'll be resurrected in the last day when everyone else will be resurrected." Do you remember what Jesus says to her in response? "I am the resurrection and the life. Whoever believes in me, though he die, yet shall he live" (John 11:17-27). This is why Paul describes Jesus as the "firstborn from the dead" (Col. 1:18) and "the first-fruits of those who have fallen asleep" (1 Cor. 15:20): Jesus Christ blazes a trail out of the grave *for us to follow*. He has paved the road that you and I will walk. He guarantees the real, physical resurrection of all people with his own real, physical resurrection. Some will be resurrected for eternal life and some will be resurrected for eternal judgment, but you can be sure of this: no person buried will stay that way (Rev. 20:11-18, 21:8; Acts 24:15; Dan. 12:2).

In the meantime, you are invited to behold him in all his beauty through his Word. Because Jesus Christ is raised from the dead, he is living and able to speak to us today through his Word. When God beckons us through Holy Scripture, it is not merely an idea we are called to contemplate, but a person with whom we are called to *commune*. Consider, then, these words from Augustine as a genuine offer, not merely rhetoric:

> Let us therefore, who believe, run to meet a Bridegroom who is beautiful where he is. Beautiful as God, as the Word who is with God, he is beautiful in the Virgin's womb, where he did not lose his godhead but assumed our humanity. Beautiful he is as a baby, as the Word unable to speak because while he was still without speech, still a baby in arms and nourished at his mother's breasts, the heavens spoke for him, a star guided the magi, and he was adored

in the manger as food for the humble. He was beautiful in heaven, then, and beautiful on earth: beautiful in the womb, and beautiful in his parent's arms. He was beautiful in his miracles but just as beautiful too in not shrinking from death, beautiful in laying down his life and beautiful in taking it up again, beautiful on the cross, beautiful in the tomb, and beautiful in heaven … Do not allow the weakness of his flesh to blind you to the splendor of his beauty. The supreme and most real beauty is justice: if you can catch him out in any injustice, you will not find him beautiful in that regard; but if he is found to be just at every point, then he is lovely in all respects. Let him come to us, so that we may gaze on him with the eyes of our spirit.[15]

Resurrected, Awaiting Resurrection

We can experience a tremendous amount of intimacy with the Trinity right now by virtue of our resurrection life. The Holy Spirit facilitates this communion offered us (John 14:18-24), and it is real and deep. But one day, the down-payment of the resurrection life we enjoy now spiritually God will enjoin and complete in a glorified dimension. Our resurrection life, in other words, has a bodily component we still await. The resurrection life you know now only in part you will experience in full, with a resurrected body fit for handling such ecstasy. And on that day, God will take all of the sweet moments of communion you experience in this life and will transport them to a higher plane. Where you once loved him without seeing him (1 Pet. 1:8-9), that love will merge with faith-retiring-sight. You will stand before Jesus and look upon his glorified flesh, and he will look upon yours, and you will feel absolutely no shame. You will hug him, and you will feel infinite power enfleshed in

---

15. Augustine, Exposition of Psalm 44 in *Expositions of the Psalms 33–50*; cited in King, *The Beauty of the Lord*, p. 211.

the arms of Jesus embracing you. Your eyes will well with tears of joy and gratitude and relief, and he will tenderly reach a hand to your face and wipe your cheek. You will open your mouth and choke out a "thank you," and he will say, "Come, sit down. This seat is yours. Let's eat."

* * *

Our Triune God, we praise you for the indescribable gift of resurrection. Where would we be if not for the resurrection of our Lord Jesus Christ? We would be dead in our trespasses, without hope or consolation that our rugged path will end anywhere but in the grave. And yet—what glorious grace!—we have been united to our Beautiful Shepherd, who has not only laid his life down for us, but has taken it up again, granting us resurrection life. Lord Jesus, in you, we live this new life now, and in you, we shall be raised again in glory. You who are the firstfruits are the guarantee of our own resurrection. We look to no one else to forge a way out of the grave. We look to no other man for the salvation of our souls than the God-man—born of the virgin Mary, marked by the perfection of an actively obedient life, suffering as the spotless Lamb of God to take away the sins of the world, and vindicated by his glorious resurrection. All praise be unto you, Lord Jesus. Amen.

6

The Ascension

Christ, the Prophet-Priest-King

"How tall is Jesus?" This is a question a colleague of mine loves to ask in theological interviews. He posed this question to me when I was interviewing for my current job, and it struck me, initially, just as odd as it probably strikes you. It's something of a trick question. You may *think* the question involves attempting to determine the height of a historical figure who lived 2,000 years ago, which would involve the biological and anthropological data necessary to determine how tall people were in that region during that time, but you'd be wrong. The essence of the question comes down to that word, "is." "How tall *is* Jesus?" You can't answer that question without assuming the answer to the *real question*—is Jesus's incarnation ongoing? Is he still, in his human nature, physically located? Is he *somewhere*? The answer is yes. Luke records the ascension of Christ in Luke 24:50-53 and Acts 1:6-11, and the New Testament in several places predicts the *bodily* return of Christ (e.g., Acts 17:31; John 5:22-27; 1 Thess. 4:17; Rev. 19:11-16). Christ's incarnation is ongoing—when the Word became flesh, he dwelt among humanity in an irreversible way. He

will *forever* be the God-man. This means that Christ, as a human, is *somewhere*, since to be a human means, in part, to be bound to spatiality. He did not ascend to enter into a kind of disembodied state only to resume a bodily existence at some point in the future—he *is* the God-man. The particulars of Jesus's location is something altogether beyond our comprehension right now. He is a man, but he is a *glorified* man, whose body is an imperishable and spiritual body (1 Cor. 15:35-49), and while its "spiritual" character does not render it nonphysical, it *does* render it incomprehensible at the present for people with non-glorified, perishable, natural bodies like us.

So, Christ is ascended as an actual human being. He will return as an actual human being. What does that *mean* for us who live out our days on this earth in the meantime? What does his ascension accomplish and how does it affect the way we relate to Christ *now*? These are the questions that concern us in this chapter. Here, I wish to show how Christ's beauty is put on dazzling display in his ascension.

The Ascension

Ascension Day is a part of the historic Christian liturgical calendar, and it marks the fortieth day from Paschal Sunday (or Easter). This falls on a Thursday, so the Sunday following Ascension Day, is Ascension Sunday. This day commemorates Christ's ascension, which occurred forty days after his resurrection. Few evangelical churches even *know* about Ascension Sunday, let alone observe it. For the most part, very little of the liturgical calendar has made its way into most evangelical churches, with the general exception of Easter and Christmas, and perhaps Good Friday and Advent. Of all the special days on the liturgical calendar, Ascension Sunday is one of the more obscure ones. While not a few of my own

friends might disagree with me, I consider this rejection of almost the entire liturgical calendar to be lamentable.

While believers should not be conscience-bound to adhere strictly to the calendar, and some elements are less desirable than others because of their overt Roman Catholic roots and theological connotations (such as Ash Wednesday), there is something appropriate about shaping a yearly calendar around the gospel story. We will have to shape our annual calendar around *something*. What could be a better alternative than orienting our calendars and schedules around the events of the gospel: Advent and Christmas leading up to the New Year to commemorate the incarnation of our Lord, followed by Holy Week and Paschal to commemorate his perfect atoning death and resurrection, followed by Ascension Sunday to commemorate his session at the right hand of the Father, and then Pentecost Sunday to commemorate the arrival of the Spirit to apply the work of Christ and sweep the Church up into the gospel story. Of course, all these things should occupy the attention and contemplation and worship of believers all throughout the year, but there is something altogether fitting, I believe, about shaping our yearly routines and rhythms according to the mold of the gospel story. Regardless of what you think about such a proposal in its entirety, I propose evangelicals strongly consider at least adding Ascension Sunday to their very small liturgical calendar.

Why make this request? Because the Ascension of Christ is a necessary, though oft-forgotten aspect of Christ's ministry in the gospel. The gospel story—the gravitational centrality of our lives—would not be complete without the ascension. This doctrine is not an afterthought; it is an essential element to Christ's work of salvation, and we minimize it to our own detriment. If Christ did not ascend to the right hand of the

Father, his atoning work would be incomplete, we would have no efficient intercessor, and we would be deprived of the Holy Spirit—which means we would still be dead in our trespasses. While there are many ways we could examine this precious doctrine, I'd like to do this by considering how Christ's ascension relates to his trifold office as our Prophet, Priest, and King (also known as the *munus triplex*, in Latin).[1]

Christ Our Ascended Prophet

Christ's role as our Prophet is a topic not altogether neglected in evangelical circles, but most considerations of his prophetic work focus on his teaching and preaching ministry in the gospel narratives. While such an aspect of Christ's prophetic office is gloriously important, I'm afraid we do not often consider how Christ occupies his role in the office of Prophet *right now*. We must remember that Christ did not stop his prophetic ministry when he ascended to heaven. He *continues* to speak authoritatively to his people, even while his mode of proclamation has changed.

How does he do this? The answer comes with the biblical resolution of a tension developed by Christ during his *earthly* prophetic ministry. In John 10, when Jesus develops his famous theological metaphor of Christ as the Good Shepherd, he writes about a future day when his sheepfold will include both Jewish *and* Gentile sheep in the same flock: "And I have other sheep that are not of this fold. I must bring them also, and they will listen to my voice. So there will be one flock, one shepherd" (John 10:16). These "other" sheep, Jesus says, will be wooed into his fold when they "listen to his voice." So,

---

1. Patrick Schreiner likewise considers the doctrine of Christ's ascension through this tri-office lens. See Patrick Schreiner, *The Ascension of Christ: Recovering a Neglected Doctrine* (Bellingham, WA: Lexham Press, 2020).

John has our attention when, two chapters later, he describes how some Greeks come to Christ, seeking an audience with him. "Now among those who went up to worship at the feast were some Greeks. So these came to Philip, who was from Bethsaida in Galilee, and asked him, 'Sir, we wish to see Jesus'" (John 12:20-21). *"Surely, this is it!"* we might think, "this must be the moment where Jesus speaks to his gentile sheep to bring them in." But we would be wrong, because Jesus's response is to *deny* their request for an audience with him. "The hour" he says, "has not come for the Son of Man to be glorified. Truly, truly, I say to you, unless a grain of wheat falls into the earth and dies, it remains alone; but if it dies, it bears much fruit" (John 12:24-25). *That is a strange response.* What does a grain of wheat falling into the earth and dying and bearing much fruit have to do with the request of these Greeks to speak with Jesus?

As we read on, Jesus gives his answer: "And I, when I am lifted up from the earth, will draw *all people* [i.e., Jews *and* Gentiles] to myself" (John 12:32). "Ah!" we think, "alright. Jesus won't draw Gentiles to himself until he is lifted up on the cross in the crucifixion. This is how he's a seed: he's got to be buried before he can sprout and bear *Gentile* fruit." And this is *almost* right, but it's not the whole story. If it were, you would expect for Jesus, upon his resurrection, to say to Philip, "Ok, Philip, go get those Greeks; I'm ready to speak to them now." But he doesn't. He spends forty days talking to *his disciples* in particular instances, and then he ascends into the heavens. And we're left scratching our heads. *When does Jesus speak to his Gentile sheep? When does he draw them into the sheepfold?* And the answer is: *right now.* He does precisely this as our ascended Prophet.

Think about the gravity of Paul's words to the Corinthians: "Therefore, we are ambassadors for Christ, God making his

appeal through us. We implore you on behalf of Christ, be reconciled to God" (2 Cor. 5:20). That's how Christ calls out to his sheep among the nations: he does it through the proclamation of his saints. When we proclaim the gospel, and when people respond, it is because they recognize in *our* words, the voice of their Good Shepherd. This is why Paul can say to the Ephesians (Gentile believers who did not come to faith until long after Christ ascended), Christ "came and preached peace to you who were far off and peace to those who were near" (Eph. 2:17). When exactly did Christ come to the Ephesians to speak peace to them? When Paul came to Ephesus with Priscilla and Aquila and proclaimed the gospel there (Acts 18:18-21). In hearing the gospel presented by Paul and his missionary companions, they heard their Good Shepherd calling out to them, and they responded to his wooing message of peace. Christ spoke through his saints to multiply his saints. He speaks through his saints to multiply his saints.

On this note, I invite you to marvel with me at the grace of our Good Shepherd to call out to us and to *woo* us with his voice. It is worth mentioning that the same word translated in John 10 as "good" is also translated as "beautiful." It is not a stretch, therefore, to translate Christ as saying, "I am the *Beautiful* Shepherd." And honestly, that translation makes just as much sense. Did we not respond to our Beautiful Shepherd when he called to us? *Do* we not respond when he calls to us now? In sermons, in songs, in Scripture, in prayer, in conversation? His sheep hear his voice and they *recognize* the goodness and the beauty therein. They are *wooed* by him. Those who heed this invitation to come to Christ for the first time recognize the loveliness of his call and they cannot resist it. They think, "*This* is the voice I have

been waiting for my whole life to hear. I was searching for this voice and I never even knew it."

This much is testified to in Scripture itself. Consider Paul's instructions in Romans 10:14 when he writes, "How then will they call on him in whom they have not believed? And how are they to believe in him of whom they have never heard? And how are they to hear without someone preaching?" Here, while I do not encourage this as a habit, I have to object to the ESV's translation here. In this instance, it seems like the New American Standard Bible gets the right idea: "How are they to believe in Him whom they have not heard?" In other words, Paul is not asking how people might believe in Jesus without hearing *about* him, but rather how people might believe in Jesus without *hearing him*. In this instance, Paul is assuming that *Christ* is speaking through the proclamation of the preacher! This is in agreement with what Paul likewise writes to the Ephesians, when he reminds them that Christ "came and preached peace to you who were far off and peace to those who were near" (Eph. 2:17). When exactly did that happen? Do we read in the gospels of Jesus traveling to Ephesus and preaching peace there? No, of course not. According to Paul, when the gospel came to Ephesus for the first time, *Christ* thus came and preached *through* the preaching of his followers.

In all this, we see that Christ still speaks. He speaks through his saints, who speak as ambassadors to a lost and dying world, so that when unbelievers are transferred from the domain of darkness into the Kingdom of God's beloved Son, it is because they have heard—in the voice of believers—the voice of their Good Shepherd and have responded appropriately. He speaks, preeminently, when his saints gather for worship to receive his Word as it is proclaimed. When a pastor stands up, filled with the Spirit of

God, proclaiming the Spirit-inspired Word of God addressed to the gathered people of God, cosmic events are taking place: there, the Bridegroom speaks tenderly to his Bride and the Good Shepherd calls out to his sheep. "Thus sayeth the Lord," is no homiletical flourish.

Christ Our Ascended Priest

"He is the radiance of the glory of God and the exact imprint of his nature, and he upholds the universe by the word of his power. After making purification for sins, he sat down at the right hand of the Majesty on high" (Heb. 1:3). This is how the author of Hebrews begins his sermon. And here, in this verse, we see a summary of what he is going to elaborate on throughout the rest of Hebrews. Jesus, the Great High Priest of God, offers atonement for the sins of his people, and then *he sits down.*

The work of atonement is the central act associated with the priestly office because the priest is responsible for standing between a holy God and his sinful people. The respective station of these two parties poses a problem that only atonement can solve: on the one side you have God—infinite in his perfection and righteousness; all-holy, without an imperfection or fault or deficiency in him—and on the other side you have his people—sinful and stubborn and defiled by their wickedness and uncleanness. How can these two parties co-exist? The answer is atonement: the guilt and uncleanness of sinful man must be paid for, cleansed, and cleared away in order for God to vindicate his holiness in his fellowship with them. That's what atonement is for as we've seen throughout this book. It is the payment of guilt. The cleansing of defilement.

Think, once, of God's instruction to the people of Israel at the beginning of the Bible, in Leviticus 16, where he

describes the Day of Atonement. On this day, an elaborate ceremony would take place, in which Israel's high priest would enter into the Most Holy Place of the tabernacle—the Holy of holies, the place in the center which was veiled from everyone else in the nation, and even the high priest was only allowed to enter in once a year—and he would come into this space, "not without blood, which he offers for himself and for the unintentional sins of the people" (Heb. 9:7). The priest would go through an elaborate ceremony which consisted of sacrificing a bull and a goat in the outer courts and taking their blood into the Holy of Holies to atone for his own sins first (Lev. 16:11) and the sins of the people second (Lev. 16:15). Blood would even cleanse the instruments of worship (which had apparently become defiled by their being used by sinful men throughout the year) (Lev. 16:18-19). One goat would be sacrificed to illustrate *propitiation* (the bloodguilt of sin had to have wrath poured out on it), and another, after the priest had confessed the sins of the people with his hand on its head signifying imputation, would be sent out into the wilderness to illustrate *expiation* (the stain of sin had to be removed) (Lev. 16:6-10; 20-28). And much more.

At every step of this elaborate ceremonial process, it was as if God was saying, "You may not come near me as you are. There is a veil between us, and you better not cross that line without *blood* to account for your wickedness. We can have no natural fellowship; I am holy and your wicked, I am pure and you are filthy, I am righteous and you are guilty!" That's the situation for which atonement accounts.

Atonement is therefore *the* central work that Christ performs as our High Priest. All the atoning work of Israel's priests were but shadows of the true substance of what Christ would accomplish. They were pointers and signs and promises. And they testified to their own inadequacy by

their perpetuity: the fact that this ceremony had to reoccur every year, performed by priest after priest, demonstrated that it was not the ultimate solution to the problem of sin. It wasn't the ultimate atonement to sin. It was rather a promise of an atonement that Christ would accomplish.

Many Christians know this much, but what we often forget is that this atoning work was not completed with Christ's death and resurrection. The cross was the altar upon which he—the Lamb of God—was slain. That's where the sacrificial Lamb was executed. But on the Day of Atonement, the high priest would sacrifice the bull and goat on the alter in the outer courts and *then he would take that blood* and enter the Holy of Holies. *That* is where atonement is made. The same is true for Christ. As High Priest, he offered up the sacrifice of his own self on the cross, but when Christ ascended to heaven, he was completing his atoning work as our Great High Priest. He was taking that blood into the heavenly Holy of Holies. So says the author of Hebrews:

> But when Christ appeared as a high priest of the good things that have come, then through the greater and more perfect tent (not made with hands, that is, not of this creation) he entered once for all into the holy places, not by means of the blood of goats and calves but by means of his own blood, thus securing an eternal redemption. For if the blood of goats and bulls, and the sprinkling of defiled persons with the ashes of a heifer, sanctify for the purification of the flesh, how much more will the blood of Christ, who through the eternal Spirit offered himself without blemish to God, purify our conscience from dead works to serve the living God (Heb. 9:11-14).

When Christ ascended, he "brought with him" his own blood to atone for our sins. And when he did that, Hebrews 1:3 says, *he sat down*. Why did he sit down? Because he was *done*. He had done with a single offering—the offering of himself—

what the endless sacrifices of the Old Testament priests could never do: he made actual purification for sins. His work was sufficient. No more yearly Days of Atonement. In the ascension, Christ completes the work of atonement. In doing so, his priestly work is intercessory. Having offered up the single, sufficient atoning sacrifice, he now appeals to that sacrifice in his *ongoing* ministry as our priestly Mediator.

The Bible is full of examples of such intercessory mediation. In Genesis, we see Abraham *interceding* for the people of Sodom and Gomorrah (Gen. 18:22-33). In Exodus, Moses intercedes for Israel (Exod. 33:12-23). And the Old Testament system of priests were a formalized way for the priests to intercede for the people of God—that's what they were doing in their sacrifices: they were appealing to God on behalf of the people with *blood*. They were standing in front of the people, in the presence of God, pleading their case. And now, according to the author of Hebrews, Christ assumes that role for *his* people, perfectly.

The former priests [i.e., intercessors, mediators] were many in number, because they were prevented by death from continuing in office, but he holds his priesthood permanently, because he continues forever. Consequently, he is able to save to the uttermost those who draw near to God through him, since he always lives to make intercession for them. For it was indeed fitting that we should have such a High Priest, holy, innocent, unstained, separated from sinners, and exalted above the heavens. He has no need, like those high priests, to offer sacrifices daily, first for his own sins and then for those of the people, since he did this once for all when he offered up himself (Heb. 7:23-25).

The problem with every other mediator and intercessor was that (a) they couldn't live forever, (b) their offerings couldn't get the job completely done, and (c) they were

imperfect and were just as sinful as the people for which they interceded. So, there were many of them, who had to offer many sacrifices. But Jesus is perfect (so he doesn't need to offer a sacrifice for himself), his sacrifice is perfect (so he doesn't need to continually offer more), and, since he is resurrected and ascended, he never dies (so he will never be succeeded by another priest). The ascension means that Jesus is, right now, before his Father, *representing his saints to him*, perfectly on account of his blood. This is illustrated beautifully by Charles Wesley, in his hymn, "Arise, My Soul, Arise:"

> Five bleeding wounds he bears
> Received on Calvary
> They pour effectual prayers
> They strongly plead for me
> "Forgive him, oh, forgive!" they cry
> "Forgive him, oh, forgive!" they cry
> "Nor let that ransomed sinner die."[2]

The ascension means that Jesus Christ is not some far off, distant figure from the past. The ascension means that his priestly office is an ongoing reality. Jesus didn't rise from the dead and simply leave us to our own devices: he rose from the dead to assume his role as our Mediator. He is, right now, interceding for his people. Which means the Christ's forgiveness is impenetrably secure because it is held fast by Jesus Christ himself. As long as he is your intercessor, you cannot be lost. The worst thing that could possibly happen to an intercessor is death, and we've already seen what happens when Jesus goes toe to toe with death. We have an intercessor who cannot be killed, and lives forever. If you are in Christ by faith, that means that your name is ever on the lips of Jesus as he intercedes for you.

---

2. Charles Wesley, *Arise, My Sou, Arise* (1742).

One of the ongoing evidences of Christ's high priestly ministry, is the presence of the Holy Spirit. Recall Jesus's words to his disciples in John 16. These are the final moments Jesus spends with his disciples before his crucifixion and he comforts them with promises and assurances. One of those promises is the impending arrival of the Holy Spirit. He says, "But now I am going to him who sent me, and none of you asks me, 'Where are you going?' But because I have said these things to you, sorrow has filled your heart. Nevertheless, I tell you the truth: it is to your advantage that I go away, for if I do not go away, the Helper will not come to you. But if I go, I will send him to you (John 16:5-7).

We learn from this passage that the ascension is necessary for the disciples to receive the Holy Spirit. This is because the presence of the Holy Spirit is a benefit of Christ's high priestly office. His role as our New Covenant Mediator is not only to make atonement for our sins, but also to send his Holy Spirit to us—the chief blessing of the New Covenant he cuts with the offering of his own blood. So, when Jesus tells his disciples, "It's better for you if I leave," he's saying, "If I don't leave, you don't get to have the Holy Spirit indwell you, because it's only when I appeal to my blood-sacrifice in heaven that that happens. I will have to physically leave you so that I can complete my duties as your High Priest and you can receive this gift of the Holy Spirit." Christ purchased the gift of the Holy Spirit for his people with blood, and part of his priestly office is to retrieve that benefit for us in the ascension to thereafter send to us.

Now, the question is, what makes the Holy Spirit such an amazing gift? Why is having him inside us better than merely having Jesus beside us? Though there is much to say in answer to this question, here are four benefits we receive from the Holy Spirit, which is made possible on account of Christ's ascension.

The Holy Spirit regenerates us and activates our faith

We see this idea in John 3:1-15, in Jesus's conversation with Nicodemus, as well as in 2 Corinthians 3:12-18, and Titus 3:4-7. Without the ministry of the Holy Spirit to give us eyes to see the worth of Christ, *none of us would be saved.* None of us would freely cling to Christ by faith because we would all remain dead in our trespasses, blinded by the veil of Satan, and slaves to our sin. It is the work of the Holy Spirit to give us new life, and to open our spiritual eyes, and to awaken our faith to receive Christ. None of that happens without the Holy Spirit, and the reception of the Holy Spirit is a benefit of Christ's high priestly work, which he completes in the ascension. Until Christ ascends to the right hand of the Father, he cannot send his Spirit to regenerate us. And until he sends his Spirit to regenerate us, we cannot be saved.

The Holy Spirit illuminates the Word of God

In 2 Corinthians 3:12–4:6, we learn that those who read the Scriptures and do not in them see the glory of Christ are impeded by a satanic veil. The glory of Christ objectively emanates from the whole Bible, but the natural man cannot see that glory until he is freed from the veil by the liberating ministry of the Holy Spirit ("where the Spirit of the Lord is, there is freedom"). The Holy Spirit illuminates God's Word to show us what is truly there: the glory of God in the face of Jesus Christ. This is the primary and definitive way that God speaks to his Church today: the Holy Spirit gives us ears to hear and eyes to see the truth of God's Word.

The Holy Spirit convicts us of sin

We learn this explicitly from John 16:8, when Christ says that the Holy Spirit will come to "convict the world concerning sin and righteousness and judgment." This is a description of

the Spirit's ministry in the world, and to the degree that we have the world in our hearts, it applies directly to us. Have not all believers experienced this? Have we not experienced the Holy Spirit's kind and firm method of utilizing our conscience to trouble us? Have we not experienced the Spirit chastise and correct us and compel us to confess and repent? And this is a grand benefit—one for which we ought to praise him! *Of course*, it is unpleasant to experience the embarrassment of being found out by the Holy Spirit—the feeling of being scorned for doing what we know we ought not do, or for failing to do that which we know we ought. It's not pleasant to feel the convicting ministry of the Spirit, who is grieved and outraged that we have given his sworn enemy—our own sin—safe passage into *his* dwelling place— our hearts. The sting of Spirit-utilized conscience hurts, of course! But what is the alternative? Affirming us in our sin, which is self-destructive and dishonoring to God? No, he loves us too much to affirm that which grieves him and destroys us. A true friend and Helper and Comforter indeed is the Holy Spirit, who doesn't allow us to sit comfortably in our sin.

Fourth, the Holy Spirit unites us to Christ and empowers our obedience.

All of the blessings we have in the gospel we have by virtue of our union with Christ. "In him" are we "blessed with every spiritual blessing in the heavenly places" (Eph. 1:3). The Spirit himself is the one who supernaturally unites us to Christ so that all the work of redemption he accomplishes on our behalf is applied to us by virtue of our union to him (Eph. 1:13-14; 2:18; 1 Cor. 12:13). In this way, when the Spirit unites us to this beautiful man by his baptism, he is baptizing us into the ocean of Triune life, and light, and love. Christ, who has eternally been given to have "life in himself"

(John 5:26) can share what he has. He who ever lives in the infinite blessedness of divine joy takes on a human nature so that humans might be incorporated by grace into what is his by nature. When the Spirit binds us to the man Christ Jesus, he thusly binds us to the meeting ground of heaven and earth: divine joy embodied. In Christ, therefore, we are brought into the infinite beatitude of God as begraced participants. And because we are, by the ministry of the Spirit, attached to the vine of Christ, we are enabled to produce Christlike fruit (John 15; Gal. 5:22-25). The promised ministry of the Holy Spirit was never supposed to apply the work of Christ to us in such a way as to give us an escape hatch to shirk his commands. That is not what Christ died for. Christ's ascended, intercessory ministry means not only that our sins have been atoned for, but also that we have the Holy Spirit indwelling us to empower our obedience. The gospel was never intended to remove the problem of disobedience by dropping the demand for obedience, but was rather intended to solve the problem of disobedience by enabling obedience.

To simply say, "Christ is interceding for me, his obedience is imputed to me, therefore no longer do I need to obey him. I can live like hell without a care in the world because Christ has done everything for me" is a gross perversion of the gospel's logic. A truly faithful gospel logic rather sounds like this, "Christ is interceding for me. His obedience is imputed to me. My sins have been atoned for. And my obedience has been purchased with his blood—he has proven it by sending his Spirit to indwell me to empower me to walk in obedience and holiness. Because of the work of Christ, I am no longer a slave to my sin, and I am free to obey him joyfully."

Christ Our Ascended King

Jesus is King. He is the promised King who would be a "son of David" to sit on David's throne forever (2 Sam. 7:1-17; see

Matt 1:1; Rom 1:3-4). Jesus's Kingship is an overwhelming theme of the four gospels, in one way or another. Patrick Schreiner notes, "All the Gospel writers label Jesus as king, though at times this attribution is indirect."[3] This means that Jesus was *born* a King and was *designated* a King during his earthly ministry. But when was he *installed* as King? The resurrection and ascension. When Christ ascended up into the heavens, he was ascending to his heavenly coronation. He was entering into what we call his "session"—having sat down, he now exercises lordship in his ongoing rule. There are several places in the Scriptures that speak helpfully on this point. One such place is found in Psalm 2:6-9.

> "As for me, I have set my King
>   on Zion, my holy hill."
> I will tell of the decree:
> The LORD said to me, "You are my Son;
>   today I have begotten you.
> Ask of me, and I will make the nations your heritage,
>   and the ends of the earth your possession.
> You shall break them with a rod of iron
>   and dash them in pieces like a potter's vessel."

The most pressing question comes down to the speaker. Who's talking here? What is this decree? Who are the characters? On the most basic level, David is referring to himself. *He* is a King whom Yahweh has set on his holy hill to take dominion of Israel's enemies. And yet, because of the lofty language and the way this passage is so frequently quoted by New Testament authors (e.g. Acts 13:33; Heb. 1:5; 5:5), it's clear that on some level, "My Son" in this passage is ultimately referring to Jesus—the Second person of the Trinity. But what does it mean that the LORD says to him,

---

3. Schreiner, *The Ascension of Christ*, p. 77.

"today I have begotten you?" What is this "begetting?" What is this "today?"

In the New Testament, several events in Christ's life reflect, or appeal to, this "conversation." The miraculous conception and birth of Christ is one event that makes theological use of this idea. The Gospel accounts of Jesus's baptism make use of it, when the Father speaks audibly to declare "This is my beloved Son, in whom I am well pleased" (Matt. 3:17; Mark 1:11; Luke 3:22; John 1:34). The moment Jesus shares with Peter, James, and John on the Mount of Transfiguration is another (Matt. 17:9-13; Mark 9:2-13; Luke 9:28-36). Jesus himself seems to appeal to this passage in his commissioning of his followers immediately before his ascension: "All authority in heaven and on earth has been given to me. Go therefore and make disciples of all nations …" (Matt. 28:19-19). In Romans 1:4 and in Acts 13:33, Paul quotes this verse in relation to Christ's resurrection, as support to God keeping his promise. And then the author of Hebrews quotes this verse as evidence of Christ's supremacy over angels (Heb. 1:5), and again to refer to God's appointment of Christ as High Priest (Heb. 5:5).

What are we to make of all these dizzying references to Psalm 2:7? Is this verse describing the physical birth of Jesus, the Son of Mary; is it talking about God's vindication of his identity at his baptism; is it talking about the same at his transfiguration; is it talking about his vindication as the Messiah in his resurrection; or is it talking about the ascension, when he is seated on the throne at the right hand of the Ancient of Days to receive all authority in heaven and on earth? The answer is: *yes and no.*

At the most transcendent level, verses 7-9 of Psalm 2 are a poetic dramatization of the pretemporal relation of the Father to the Son. One scholar notes that "for the earliest

Christians, Psalm 2:7 was consistently regarded not merely as a direct speech made by the Father to the Son, but rather it was taken as *a speech within a speech that was originally spoken by the Son*, who was reporting the words the *Father had spoken to him at an earlier time.*[4] In other words, David is reenacting the Son, who retells of this pretemporal, eternal conversation with the Father. So, David says, "I will tell of the decree:" and then he embodies the Son, saying, "In the timeless eternity of our Triune fellowship, the LORD said to me [the eternal Son], 'You are my Son, today I have begotten you.'" This is a divine dramatization to illustrate the awe-inspiring doctrine we call eternal generation, which we have already considered at some length in this book. The Father is eternally the Father *of the* Son—this "today" is a timelessly eternal "today." Never was there a time that the Father began to generate the Son, and never was there a time that the Son was not generated by the Father. Like how the source of a light is indiscernible apart from the light it generates, so the Father must be understood eternally as the Father *of the Son*. This is why the author of Hebrews calls the Son, "the *radiance*" of the Father (Heb. 1:3). A light and its radiance are not different in their essence; they are mutually defining.

But that's not all that this passage tells us. The Son's speech is not over, for he goes on to announce how the Father gives this invitation: "Ask of me, and I will make the nations your heritage, and the ends of the earth your possession. You shall break them with a rod of iron and dash them in pieces like a potter's vessel" (v. 8-9). Because the Son is the eternally begotten Son of the Father, the nations are his heritage. And this means that what the Triune God does *in time* is

---

4. Matthew W. Bates, *The Birth of the Trinity: Jesus, God, and Spirit in New Testament and Early Christian Interpretations of the Old Testament* (New York, NY: Oxford University Press, 2016), p. 64. Emphasis added.

a fitting *reflection* of what is true of the timeless eternity of his "today."

The virgin conception and birth of Christ, his baptism, his transfiguration, and his resurrection are all fitting reflections of what this conversation teaches us about: the Son is the eternally begotten one. The one who is *from* the Father and is therefore heir to the nations. In *every* stage of the gospel, therefore, Christ is revealing that he is the one about whom Psalm 2 speaks.

Advent is therefore the beginning of the Son claiming what is rightfully his. When he came in humble form as a babe in Bethlehem, he was coming to claim the nations. And he does this in the most counterintuitive way: he assumes a weak and fragile nature. The incarnation is a magnificent display of God shaming the wisdom of the wise with divine folly. It is baffling, awe-inspiring, and beautiful. This is how he begins to claim his heritage of the nations—he comes in humility and kindness to fetch them. By the time his Davidic identity is vindicated and *declared* by his resurrection, he is ready to ascend into heaven to receive the honor the Father promised to David's heir: universal dominion over the nations. To see this drama unfold, we have to look to *another* Old Testament passage. In Daniel 7, the prophet Daniel receives a vision that Christ will explicitly claim as his own.

> I saw in the night visions,
> and behold, with the clouds of heaven
> there came one like a son of man,
> and he came to the Ancient of Days
> and was presented before him.
> And to him was given dominion
> and glory and a kingdom,
> that all peoples, nations, and languages
> should serve him;

> his dominion is an everlasting dominion,
> which shall not pass away,
> and his kingdom one
> that shall not be destroyed.
> (Dan. 7:13-14; see also Matt. 26:64; Mark 14:62)

It's very common for people to assume that this passage is describing Christ's *return*; that he will come on the clouds *to earth* with his angels to bring judgment against his enemies and to realize his universal dominion on earth. As we'll see momentarily, such a return *is* a promise to which Christians ought to cling. But Daniel 7:13-14 is *not* talking about the return of Christ; it's talking about his *ascension*. He does not ride on the clouds to *earth*, but rather into the heavenly presence of "the Ancient of Days." "Ask of me and I will give you the nations" (Ps. 2:8), says the Father in Psalm 2, and in Daniel 7 we read, "and to him was given a dominion and glory and kingdom, that all peoples, nations and languages should serve him" (Dan. 7:13) and "all authority in heaven and on earth has been given to me, go therefore and make disciples of all nations" (Matt. 28:18-19) should all be read together. When Christ was resurrected, his office as the Davidic King who would perpetually reign was *vindicated* and *declared*, but upon his ascension, this reign *began*. The fruit of his dominion, right now, is none other than the steady victorious advance of the gospel across the globe. The nations are being discipled, slowly and surely, like leaven filling a loaf or a mustard seed growing to a tree (Matt. 13:24-33).

Paul declares as much when he says, "For he must reign until he has put all his enemies under his feet. The last enemy to be destroyed is death" (1 Cor. 15:25-26). Right now, Jesus Christ has been installed in his heavenly rule. One of the ways he demonstrates his reign on earth is through his heavenly embassies: local churches, those local expressions

of the universal Church who are endowed with King Jesus's keys (Matt. 16:19; 18:18-20). He is the head of the Church (Col. 1:18), and his kingly dominion is discernible now chiefly through those who live according to his authoritative commands. He *is* king over all the nations right now, even if his kingship is not yet as discernible as it will be in the age to come. But make no mistake: creation has a King, and his name is Jesus.

Sidebar 6.1
One Divine Will

Because the three persons of the Trinity share in one, simple, divine nature, they share in one, simple, divine power and will. In other words, the Trinity is not a society of three separate divine wills acting in unison together, as if there were three separate willers with three separate centers of consciousness. Since there is one divine nature, so too there is one divine power and will.

Christ Our Returning King

One day, our present state of "already/not yet" will shed its "not yet" character. Christ will return, bodily, to make all things new and to bring human history to its glorious climax. We refer to this doctrine as the *Parousia*—the "appearing" of Christ. "For the Lord himself will descend from heaven with a cry of command," says Paul, "with the voice of an archangel, and with the sound of the trumpet of God. And the dead in Christ will rise first" (1 Thess. 4:16). This scene, and those glorious features associated with it, is foretold in dramatic fashion in Revelation 19–22:5. Paul tells us that creation itself is growing for this day, when Christ returns and the sons of God are redeemed with glorified bodies, since this will signal the end of its subjection to sin and corruption (Rom. 8:18-25). "I believe in the resurrection of the body and

the life everlasting," we confess with the Apostle's Creed. "I look for the resurrection of the dead and the life of the world to come," we say with the Nicene Creed. Why is that important to remember? Because we must remember that this sustained meditation on the most beautiful man to ever live is not an exercise in a mere thought experiment. We aren't imagining what it might have been like to know Jesus *back when he lived* on this planet. Rather, we have been getting better acquainted with him whom we commune with, by the Spirit, through his Word, *now*. Further, we have been stirring our affections for one with whom we will be reunited on *this* planet, physically, where we will live in a glorified and sinless state *forever.*

> Then I saw a new heaven and a new earth, for the first heaven and the first earth had passed away, and the sea was no more. And I saw the holy city, new Jerusalem, coming down out of heaven from God, prepared as a bride adorned for her husband. And I heard a loud voice from the throne saying, "Behold, the dwelling place of God is with man. He will dwell with them, and they will be his people, and God himself will be with them as their God. He will wipe away every tear from their eyes, and death shall be no more, neither shall there be mourning, nor crying, nor pain anymore, for the former things have passed away" (Rev. 21:1-4).

No longer will we feel the ache of longing absence. While he is in our midst, communing with us, we are consigned to behold his glory with the eyes of faith. But in that day, him whom we delight to behold by faith now, we shall behold in glorified vision.[5] Every good and godly desire in this life is

---

5. For a deeper dive into this glorious doctrine of the beatific vision, see Samuel G. Parkison, *To Gaze Upon God: The Beatific Vision in Doctrine, Tradition, and Practice* (Downers Grove, IL: IVP Academic, 2024).

a road that leads *there*. We will never grow bored or tired of delighting in his presence. Every maximally joyful moment will be topped by the next, further up and further in, forever.

When the Light of the World comes to be the light within our midst, he will transfigure the cosmos with his own radiance. He who is supremely beautiful will beautify all else. Wherever our gaze rests in that happy land we will find that we are looking at the divine beauty of the Son, infused into all that he has restored in himself, when he consummates the work he began here to "reconcile all things to himself, whether on earth or in heaven" (Col. 1:20). There, where we rest in our final and everlasting Sabbath, we will be able to say the words of the psalmist more truly than ever they were said, "For with you is the fountain of light; in your light do we see light" (Ps. 36:9).

* * *

He who testifies to these things says,
"Surely I am coming soon." Amen. Come, Lord Jesus!
(Rev 22:20)

Lord Jesus, our Beautiful Prophet-Priest-King, we lift our thanks to you, knowing that you hear our prayers—for you are the resurrected, ascended, and reigning one. We know this from experience, for we continue to be guided and directed by your ongoing prophetic ministry; we enjoy the benefits of your ongoing priestly intercession with a faith still intact; and we have come to experience the liberating joy of deliverance from the domain of darkness to dwell as citizens of your Kingdom. Our Beautiful Shepherd, you feed us continually with your nourishing Word, you empower us with the blood-bought blessing of your Spirit's presence, you rule over us as our benevolent King. Lord Jesus, we lift our hearts to pray with

the innumerable saints who have gone before us, and we plead with you to make your kingdom come, that your will might be done here on earth as it is in heaven. You are King of all creation, and we long to see your dominion rightly celebrated from coast to coast, so that your beauty—which transfixes the eyes of our hearts with the sight of faith—might be the all-satisfying object of our glorified vision. So, we pray, come, Lord Jesus! Amen.

Conclusion

Throughout this book, we have been reveling in the beauty of Christ. In doing so, we have been banking on the trustworthiness of what Jonathan Edwards says here:

> So with what great delight may [those] that love Christ with an active love spend their thoughts upon his glories; with what pleasure may they meditate upon those infinite perfections that he is possessed of, and which make him lovely in their eyes. How must it please them to find out continually new beauties and glories which they saw not before, for the excellencies of Christ are infinite and we may make new discoveries to all eternity, and yet not have discovered all. How doth it fill the soul with a kind of rapture when it has discovered something more of excellency in him who is the object of his highest love.[1]

But at this point, you may be wondering about the second part of the subtitle of this book. I have suggested that we would consider "The Beautiful Christ *and His Ugly Rivals.*" Where are these rivals? In truth, I have been implicitly contrasting Christ with them throughout this book. But here at the close,

---

1. Jonathan Edwards, *Works of Jonathan Edwards*, 10:615.

it might be worth identifying and naming them explicitly to avoid any ambiguity. The real Jesus—the unvarnished Jesus who created the cosmos and holds all things together by his powerful Word and revealed himself in the incarnation, the Jesus who is proclaimed in the Scriptures, who still *speaks* through Holy Scripture, and who has been heralded and cherished and worshipped by all the orthodox throughout Christianity's Great Tradition—is infinitely more beautiful than his rival knockoffs. The following list is a non-exhaustive sampling of such counterfeit rivals.

The non-beautiful "Jesus" of a non-beautiful reality.[2]

This first rival is admittedly very abstract, but I might be so bold as to say that this is the most common rival to the real Jesus in our postmodern world. In this framework, Jesus doesn't fit into the story of the cosmos as objective apex of beauty because in this framework, beauty isn't objective at all. Beauty is purely subjective and therefore cannot have an objective *apex*. Thus, in this framework, Jesus can be called many things, but he cannot be called the absolute revelation of divine Beauty. This rival-Jesus is embarrassingly inferior to the real, beautiful Jesus of Scripture and Christian tradition because it depends on a cognitive dissonance, where our conscious beliefs about beauty run contrary to what we *know* to be true of beauty by experience. At the end of the day, we *know* that the truly grotesque is not judged to be so on a whim, arbitrarily, and that the truly beautiful cannot *merely* be considered so as a matter of taste. At the level of our souls, we know that beauty has to transcend our tiny experiences of it—it pulls and beckons and prods us beyond our experiences and tastes and subjective judgments to the level of the ineffable and untouchable Absolute. The true

---

2. See the introduction.

Jesus—the unvarnished beautiful Jesus of Christianity—is superior to this rival not only because he makes more sense of our experiences with beauty and ugliness in this world, but also because he grants us access to be united to that Absolute transcendental beauty for which we long, as our desire for that access is awakened by every experience of desire in this life. All roads of desire lead, ultimately, to their satisfaction in communion with God, and they all run through the beautiful Jesus of Holy Scripture.

The non-beautiful "Jesus" of sentimentalism.[3]

This, again, is the rival-Jesus of "Jesus-is-my-boyfriend" praise songs. This androgynous Jesus should awaken no respect or admiration, let alone *worship*, from any self-respecting Christian. This Jesus is a tame and effeminate Jesus, and he is dwarfed by the infinite majesty of the biblical Jesus we have been admiring throughout this book.

The non-beautiful "Jesus" of Arianism.[4]

This Jesus is the one who is not timelessly eternal, but was rather the first and greatest of God's creation. Such a Jesus must not be worshipped or adored, since he is not divine. The church fathers in the fourth century rightly condemned devotees of this Jesus as heretics unbecoming of the designation of "Christian," and, while there are few (if any) who would own the title of "Arianism" today, this rival-Jesus has resurfaced in a number of ways in different forms throughout the centuries. Islam, Jehovah's Witness, and Mormonism all confess belief in a "Jesus" who is, at bottom, *creature*. Over and against this pathetic rival-Jesus, the true Jesus shines forth as the beautiful "only begotten, Son of the Father"—he is "God of God, Light of Light, Very

---

3. See the introduction.
4. See chapter 2.

God of Very God," and as such, he deserves our admiration and adoration.

The non-beautiful "Jesus" of kenoticism.[5]

Kenoticism takes its name from the Greek word *kenosis*—or self-emptying—which Paul uses to describe the incarnation in Philippians 2:7. This rival-Jesus is one who divests himself of something divine in the incarnation. Strong kenoticists may go so far as to say that Jesus left the divine nature entirely behind when he was incarnate, while weaker versions—or *functional* kenoticists—will say that he simply divested himself of divine prerogatives. But either way, such rival-Jesuses pale in comparison to the unvarnished Jesus of orthodox Christianity, since they cannot but diminish the beauty of the divine nature. The divine nature is purely actual and infinite *Life*. There is no such thing as "partial" divinity, or "divinity un-used" or any such thing like that. The divine nature is infinitely vivacious—simple and pure and eternally profuse. The unvarnished Jesus of Christian orthodoxy outshines the rival-Jesus of kenoticism precisely because he retains and reveals what the kenoticists insist he left behind: *infinite divine beauty!*

Sidebar Conclusion.1
Pure Actuality

This doctrine affirms that God has no passive potency—meaning, God has no potential to become anything that he is not already. There is no *becoming* in God. If God could become, he would not be perfect. God's pure actuality means he is the *plentitude* or *fullness* of being: the fullness of life and light and love.

---

5. See chapter 2.

The non-beautiful "Jesuses" of Apollinarianism, Nestorianism, Monothelitism, and Eternal Functional Subordinationism.[6]

These rival-Jesuses are clustered together because of how they relate to one another conceptually. All of them obscure Holy Scripture's depiction of Jesus's beauty by attempting to dispel the praise-inducing mystery of the incarnation and the hypostatic union of Christ's two natures. The Apollinarian Jesus denies to the Son of God the beauty of a perfectly consecrated *human soul*—Apollinarianism will grant him a body alone. Likewise, the Monothelite Jesus denies to the Son of God the beauty of a perfectly obedient *human will.* The Nestorian Jesus, on the other hand, diminishes the oneness of a Jesus who is hypostatically united to both a human and divine nature. The Jesus of Eternal Functional Subordinationism (EFS) diminishes the glory of Jesus by diminishing his power and authority—this portrayal of Jesus defines his Sonship not—as Scripture and tradition insists— solely based on his eternal relation of origin to the Father as being eternally generated, but rather by the function of submission he renders the Father. In this portrayal, the Son's glory is a lesser glory to the Father's, and his authority is a lesser authority. The divine Son of EFS is not a subsistence of the one, simple divine nature, but is rather one *willer* of a society of divine persons, whose will is always—by definition—in subjection to another divine will.[7] The biblical

---

6. See chapter 2.

7. For more on this erroneous model of the Trinity, see Matthew Barrett, *Simply Trinity: The Unmanipulated Father, Son, and Spirit* (Grand Rapids, MI: Baker Books, 2021); Matthew Barrett, Ronni Kurtz, Samuel G. Parkison, and Joseph Lanier, *Proclaiming the Triune God: The Doctrine of the Trinity in the Life of the Church* (Nashville, TN: B&H Academic, 2024), and Samuel G. Parkison, "The Trinity is *Still* Not Our Social Program: The Trinity in Gender Roles," in Matthew Barrett (ed.)

Jesus, however, is a mystery—a magnificent, glorious, heart-stopping mystery: truly God and truly man, with a rational soul and human flesh. He is the beauty of man—perfect, holy, and obedient. All that is truly beautiful in humanity—including the moral beauty of a human will absolutely consecrated to God in worship—Jesus reveals. Likewise, all that is truly beautiful of the divine, Jesus reveals. And he does all this revealing of divine and human beauty as truly *one*.

Sidebar Conclusion.2
Eternal Functional Subordination

Eternal Functional Subordination (EFS) or Eternal Roles of Authority and Submission (ERAS) is a novel model of trinitarianism created in the latter part of the twentieth century. EFS is a kind of social trinitarianism that affirms the ontological equality of the three persons of the Trinity, but distinguishes the persons within the in the inner life of God not solely according to their eternal processions, but rather also according to their functional roles of authority and submission. Therefore, EFS presupposes three distinct divine wills and centers of consciousness in the Trinity and portrays the Trinity as something of a harmonious society of divine persons defined by hierarchical relationships. When EFS first came into popularity, its advocates either rejected, or viewed with extreme suspicion, historic orthodox affirmations about the Trinity such as the doctrine of divine simplicity, eternal generation, inseparable operations, or a single divine will. In recent years, EFS advocates have announced their acceptance to these historic affirmations, but they do so in idiosyncratic and incoherent ways, changing their fundamental and historic meanings, in order to preserve their fundamental claim that the persons of the Trinity can be defined by their authoritatively hierarchical roles. This makes EFS one of the most widely accepted *heterodoxies* (i.e., it is outside the bounds of historic, orthodox trinitarianism) in the evangelical church today.

On Classical Trinitarianism: Retrieving the Nicene Doctrine of the Triune God (Downers Grove, IL: IVP Academic, 2024).

The non-beautiful "Jesus" of "possible atonement" theories.

What makes Jesus's human beauty so irresistible is the fact that he performs his high priestly vocation in a superlative manner. He dies to save his flock, he atones for the actual sins of his people, not the possible sins of a possible people. This Jesus is more beautiful than his rival because the work he performs on behalf of his people is more beautifully effective. He sheds his blood for no one in the abstract, and his beloved Bride in the particular, and for that, his bloodshed is an infinitely beautiful display of love.[8]

* * *

I have chosen to name these rival Jesuses in such an explicit manner here at the end of the book because my desire was not to shock you into taking my claim seriously by leading with polemics, but to rather portray a positively beautiful vision of the real, unvarnished Jesus. If I have succeeded, this brief outline should not strike the reader as offensive, since the appeal of these rival conceptions of Jesus will have lost their luster in the light of the real Christ's brilliance. Other portrayals of Jesus may not be grotesque if viewed in themselves, but when compared to the dazzling beauty of the unvarnished Lord Jesus Christ, they are rendered as much by way of comparison.

---

8. For a more exhaustive defense of this doctrine, see David Gibson and Jonathan Gibson, eds., *From Heaven He Came and Sought Her: Definite Atonement in Historical, Biblical, Theological, and Pastoral Perspective* (Wheaton, IL: Crossway, 2013).

Recommended Resources

Old Books

St. Athanasius the Great of Alexandria, trans. John Behr, *On the Incarnation* (St. Vladimir's Seminary Press, 2014).

St. Thomas Aquinas, trans. Richard J. Regan, *Compendium of Theology* (Oxford University Press, 2009).

St. Cyril of Alexandria, trans. Anthony McGuckin, *On the Unity of Christ* (St. Vladimir's Seminary Press, 2005).

St. Maximus the Confessor, trans. Paul M. Blowers and Robert Louis Wilkin, *On the Cosmic Mystery of Jesus Christ* (St. Vladimir's Seminary Press, 2011).

Petrus van Mastricht, *Theoretical-Practical Theology. Vol. 2, Faith in the Triune God*, edited by Joel R. Beeke (Reformation Heritage Books, 2019).

Francis Turretin, *Institutes of Elenctic Theology, 3 vols* (P&R, 1992).

Introductory Books

Matthew Barrett, Ronni Kurtz, Samuel G. Parkison, Joseph Lanier, *Proclaiming the Triune God: The Doctrine of the Trinity in the Life of the Church* (B&H Academic, 2024).

John Murray, *Redemption Accomplished and Applied* (Eerdmans, 2015).

Scott R. Swain, *The Trinity: An Introduction* (Crossway, 2020).

Stephen J. Wellum, *The Person of Christ: An Introduction* (Crossway, 2021).

Intermediate Books

Matthew Barrett, *Simply Trinity: The Unmanipulated Father, Son, and Holy Spirit* (Baker Books, 2021).

D. Glenn Butner, *Trinitarian Dogmatics: Exploring the Grammar of the Christian God* (2022).

Brandon D. Crowe, *The Lord Jesus Christ: The Biblical Doctrine of the Person and Work of Christ* (Lexham Press, 2023).

Fred Sanders, *The Triune God* (Zondervan, 2016).

Daniel Treier, *Lord Jesus Christ* (Zondervan, 2023).

Advanced Books

Matthew Barrett (ed.), *The Doctrine on Which the Church Stands or Falls: Justification in Biblical, Theological, Historical, and Pastoral Perspective* (Crossway, 2019).

Matthew Barrett (ed.), *On Classical Trinitarianism: Retrieving the Nicene Doctrine of the Triune God* (IVP Academic, 2024).

Steven J. Duby, *Jesus and the God of Classical Theism: Biblical Christology in Light of the Doctrine of God* (Baker Academic, 2023).

Thomas Joseph White, *The Trinity: On the Nature and Mystery of the One God* (CUA, 2022).

Thomas Joseph White, *The Incarnate Lord: A Thomistic Study in Christology* (CUA, 2017).

Glossary

Accommodation refers to God's self-revelation, in which he reveals himself truly to his creatures, but since he is infinite and they are finite, he must *stoop* or *translate* or *accommodate* himself to be knowable.

Active Obedience of Christ refers to his life of positively and meritoriously obeying divine law. Because Christ *actively* obeyed for those who have been justified by faith in him, they are now positively considered *righteous*, on account of the meritorious righteousness that Christ earned and has imputed to them.

Analogy as a theological concept (whether in linguistics or metaphysics) is used to convey the likeness and unlikeness that relates creation to its Creator. Creation—and creaturely language—is always, at its best, simultaneously similar and dissimilar to God.

Apollinarianism is an ancient Christian heresy that denies that the Son took on a human soul or will when he assumed a human nature. The nature Christ assumed, in

other words, was less than truly human, because it was a body without a soul.

Arianism is an ancient Christian heresy that denies that the Son is coequal with the Father, and is rather the first and greatest of God's creatures.

Aseity refers to God's independence and self-sufficiency—he is *of himself*, and his life is not derived from another, but is rather the plentitude of divine life in and of himself.

Athanasian Creed dates back to the sixth century, two centuries after Athanasius lived (d. 373). This creed represents the culmination of Trinitarian and Christological theology developed according to orthodoxy up to that point and stress the co-eternal glory of the three persons of the Trinity, their essential oneness, as well as their distinct modes of subsistence. The creed also carefully distinguishes between the two natures of Christ united in the one person, and therefore reads as something of a combination and extrapolation of the Apostle's Creed, the Nicene Creed, and the Definition of Chalcedon. The Athanasian Creed is accepted by virtually all historic forms of Western Christianity, whether Roman Catholic or Protestant.

Atonement refers to the sacrificial act whereby God and man are reconciled. Penal substitutionary atonement teaches that this reconciliation comes as a result of Christ's sacrificial offering of his life on behalf of those whom he saves.

Chalcedon Definition is the name for a document written at an ecumenical council in the city of Chalcedon in A.D. 451. This document names and defines the relationship of

Christ's two natures (divine and human) united in the single divine person.

Christus Victor refers to the aspect of Christ's atonement that highlights his victory over Satan, death, and the demonic powers.

Communicatio Idiomatum refers, in the reformed tradition, to the communication of properties or idioms of either of Christ's natures (divine or human). Whatever can be truly said of divinity can be said of the Son, and whatever can be truly said of humanity can be said of the Son, but this does not mean that whatever can be said of humanity can be said of divinity, and vice versa. Divinity is timeless, and therefore the Son is timeless; humanity is time-bound and therefore the Son is time-bound. But the Son's humanity is not timeless, and the Son's divinity is not time-bound.

Cosmos refers to the orderly structure of all created being. "Universe" is sometimes used as a synonym for Cosmos, but whereas "the universe" often contains connotations of what exists "out there" in "outer space," Cosmos retains the connotation of an ordered, structured, interrelatedness of all creaturely existence—from the furthest distant galaxies to the tiniest molecular structure.

Covenant of Grace refers to God's covenant to undo the disaster of the covenant of works and to graciously grant forgiveness of sins and redemption to those who participate therein. Ultimately, this covenant is ratified through the gospel of Jesus Christ. Some reformed traditions teach that the Covenant of Grace existed prior to the *New Covenant* (promised in Jeremiah 31:31-34, among other passages) under a different administration (e.g., the Mosaic Covenant), while others teach that the Covenant of Grace existed prior to the New Covenant only

in a promissory fashion, and did not come into historical ratification until the death and resurrection of Christ. But in either case, participants of the Covenant of Grace receive the salvation it offers by faith in Christ alone.

Covenant of Redemption / Pactum Salutis refers to the intra-trinitarian covenant between the Father and Son (and Spirit) to redeem a Bride for Christ through the gospel. This covenant was established "before the foundation of the world."

Covenant of Works refers to the covenant God entered into with Adam and humanity in the garden of Eden. The terms were everlasting life and the beatific vision as a result of full, perfect, and complete obedience to God; but this covenant was broken when Adam took from the tree of the knowledge of good and evil.

Definite Atonement refers to the view of Christ's atonement that says that Christ did not merely die to make atonement possible, but that his atonement is made definitively for the elect. In other words, definite atonement says that Christ's atonement did not make salvation merely possible, but that it *atones for* and *saves* people.

Divine Incomprehensibility affirms the infinity of God in relation to creaturely knowledge. Though we can know God *truly*, we can never know him *comprehensively*, because he is infinite and we are finite.

Divine Will refers to God's infinite power of rationality. Since the will is an operation of nature—and not a personal property or eternal relation of origin—the divine Trinity as *one* will.

Dyothelitism refers to monothelitism's counter-position (dyo = two; thelite = will). Dyothelites affirmed that since Christ

existed in two natures, divine and human, he had to have two wills. This position was vindicated as orthodox at the sixth ecumenical council, Constantinople III (A.D. 681).

Eternal Functional Subordination or Eternal Relations of Authority and Submission (ERAS) is a novel theological position, aberrant Nicene orthodoxy, that portrays the persons of the Trinity in a hierarchical way. EFS is a conservative form of social trinitarianism that says that the persons of the Trinity are distinguished in the inner life of God—in part, at least—by their roles of authority and submission, wherein the Father has all authority, and the Son submits.

Eternal Generation refers to the Son's relation of origin. He eternally proceeds from the Father as the one who is eternally begotten (or generated) from the Father. Eternal Generation distinguishes the Son from the Father and Spirit in the inner life of God (i.e., without any reference to creation).

Eternal Processions / Eternal Relations of Origin refers to who the persons of the Trinity are in relation to each other within the timelessly eternal existence of the Godhead. These relations of origin are "unbegottenness" (i.e., the Father—his relation of origin is *as* timeless origin), "begottenness (i.e., the Son—he is eternally begotten *from* the Father), and "spiration" (i.e., the Spirit—he is eternally *spirated* or *breathed forth* from the Father [and the Son]). Importantly, the eternal processions—these eternal relations of origin—distinguish the persons of the Trinity in relation to *one another*, not in relation to *divinity proper*: each person is wholly and entirely the divine nature subsisting.

Eternal Spiration refers to the Spirit's relation of origin. He eternally proceeds from the Father (and the Son) as the one who is *breathed* out. Eternal Spiration distinguishes the Spirit from the Father and Son in the inner life of God (i.e. without any reference to creation).

Exegesis refers to proper interpretation of the text. To exegete a text is to draw out its meaning.

Expiation refers to the atonement act of removing the *stain* of sin and defilement for the one who has been atoned for.

Extra Calvinisticum is a doctrine that seeks to uphold the hypostatic union and Chalcedonian Christology by insisting on the distinction, without confusion, of Christ's two natures. This doctrine affirms that while Christ truly lives in his human nature, his person is not *contained* by that nature; he remains infinite in virtue of his divine nature, even while he is finite in virtue of his human nature.

Federal Headship refers to the covenantal mechanism whereby one person can act on behalf of the many. Adam was the federal head of humanity, and Christ—the last Adam—is the federal head of a new humanity, redeemed from the first.

Finite / Infinite are terms used to convey the Creator-creature distinction. To be finite is to be bound or limited, but to be infinite is to be altogether unbounded, unlimited, and eternal.

Hypostatic Union refers to the uniting together of Christ's two natures in the single person (with the word *hypostasis* referring to the person, God the Son, and *union* referring to both natures united to that person).

Immutability refers to God's changelessness.

Impassibility refers to God's changelessness with respect to passions or suffering.

Incarnation describes the eternal Son's assumption of a human nature.

Inseparable Operations affirms that the external works of the Trinity are undivided. Because God is one, God acts as one—because God is no less than Trinity, God's actions are always trinitarian. All of God's actions are *from* the Father and *through* the Son and *by* the Spirit.

Justification refers to the judicial act whereby God declares someone to be no longer guilty, and positively righteous. Justification, according to Scripture and the reformed tradition, is by faith alone in Christ alone.

Kenotic / Kenoticism gets its name from the Greek word *kenosis* which Paul uses this word in Philippians 2:7 to describe Christ's act of "self-emptying" in the incarnation. "Kenoticism" or "Kenotic Christology" is a theological position aberrant to Christian orthodoxy that arose in the nineteenth century, which asserts that such "self-emptying" amounts to the divine Son emptying himself of either (a) the divine nature, (b) certain divine attributes, or (c) certain divine *prerogatives* during his earthly incarnate ministry.

Monothelitism is a theological position that came under scrutiny in the seventh century. Monothelites believed that while Christ had two genuine natures (divine and human) he has one will (Mono = one; thelite = will). This position was deemed heretical at the sixth ecumenical council, Constantinople III (A.D. 681).

Nestorianism is an ancient Christian heresy that stresses the division of Christ's two natures to the neglect of their

union in the single person, such that the divine Son and the human Christ become accepted as two different subjects.

Nicene Creed is a document first written in A.D. 325 in the city of Nicaea as a result of the first ancient ecumenical council. Later, in A.D. 381, it was edited and expanded in tandem with another ecumenical council in the city of Constantinople. The Nicene Creed is concerned with naming and defending the doctrine of the Trinity.

Omnipresence refers to God's infinite spatial presence (omni = all; presence). God is infinite and limitless in every regard, including time and space. Another way of describing God's omnipresence is to refer to his infinite *immensity*.

Omnipotence refers to God's infinite power (omni = all; potency = power). God is infinite and limitless in every regard, including power.

Omniscience refers to God's infinite knowledge (omni = all; science = knowledge). God is infinite and limitless in every regard, including knowledge.

Parousia refers to the *appearing* of Christ at his second coming, at the end of this age.

Partitive Exegesis is the name given to a particular strategy for exegeting passages of Scripture that deal with Christ, so that the meaning of a given passage might cohere with what Scripture says about Christ and his two natures (divine and human) as a whole.

Passive Obedience of Christ refers to his life of suffering the consequence of divine law-breaking. He experienced the impact of the curse in a judicial way, and this passive obedience whereby he suffers the consequence of divine law-breaking culminates with his death on the cross.

Because Christ *passively* obeyed for those who have been justified by faith in him, they are *no longer guilty*—he suffered on their behalf.

Persons are defined by the church father, "Boethius," as "The individual substance of a rational nature." This is a broad enough definition to describe human persons (human nature, after all, as a composite of body and soul, is *rational*; so human persons are individual substances of human nature, which is rational) and divine persons. Each of the persons of the Trinity are individual substances of a rational nature; but the rationality (will) and nature each is a subsistence of is the selfsame. One nature, one will, three persons.

Platonism is a school of Ancient Greek philosophy named after the philosopher, Plato. Plato and the Platonic tradition is the most well-known expression of philosophical *realism*, which affirms that universals are real and not imaginary or conceptual or in name only.

Propitiation refers to the atonement act of satisfying the wrath of God in the death of Christ. Divine wrath was *propitiated* (or satisfied, or diverted, or absorbed) in Christ's substitutionary atonement.

Pure Actuality refers to God's unbounded, ceaseless life. He has no passive potency in him—meaning, he has no potential to become anything he is not already—he is rather infinitely himself eternally.

Recapitulation refers to the way he embodies and perfects, in a typological way, various people and events traced out all throughout the Old Testament. He *recapitulates,* and thereby restores in himself, the broken history of Israel in the Old Testament.

Revelation refers to God's act of *revealing* himself to his creatures. *General revelation* refers to God revealing himself through creation in general, and *special revelation* refers to God revealing himself through the acts of redemption documented in the Scriptures, as well as the Scriptures themselves.

Simple / Simplicity is the absolute denial of composition in God. He is not composed in any way: parts, passions, powers, or accidence. As such, all that is in God is God.

Summum Bonum refers to man's highest good.

Transcendentals refers to the triad of the True, the Good, and the Beautiful, are characteristics of absolute being. At the very top of the "chain of being," the True, Good, and Beautiful are all one.

Tritheism is a very specific kind of polytheism. It affirms three gods. And while no professing Christians affirm tritheism per se, tritheism seems nevertheless to be the logical conclusion of many articulations of social trinitarianism, which often stress that the unity of the Trinity is not owing primarily to a singularity of nature, but rather to a kind of societal agreement of divine wills and centers of consciousness.

Unbegotten refers to the Father's "relation of origin." He eternally generates (the Son) and eternally breathes forth (the Spirit). Eternal Unbegottenness distinguishes the Father from the Son and Spirit in the inner life of God (i.e., without any reference to creation).

Union with Christ is a doctrine that affirms that all the blessings of salvation come to the believer by virtue of being united to Christ by faith. It is *in Christ* that the believer experiences the grace of God in salvation.

Universal Atonement refers to the view of Christ's atonement that says Christ's atonement made universal salvation possible, but that actual salvation depends on whether someone places faith in Christ or not. Universal atonement says that Christ's atonement makes salvation possible for any, but does not actually save—as an act in itself—any.

Scripture Index

GENESIS

3:15 ....65, 66
3:21 108
18:22-33...................... 161
22:1-14 108
22:14 108

EXODUS

12:1-32....................... 108
33:12-23...................... 161
25:1-36......................... 36

LEVITICUS

16................105, 108, 158

DEUTERONOMY

6:4 60

2 SAMUEL

6:1-17 36
7:1-17 166
24:1-17 79

JOB

26:6 118

PSALMS

2:8 171
2:12 6
7:11.............................. 95
19:1 .... 10, 14, 21, 33
19:1-6........................... 33
19:12 108
33:6-9 33
36:9 174
139:8 118

PROVERBS

27:20 118

ISAIAH

52:13–53:12............... 108

DANIEL

7:13-14 171
12:2 148

MATTHEW

3:17 168
11:29 6
17:9-13 168
19:14 6

26:39 75
26:56 130
26:64........................... 171
27:50 70
28:18-19.............. 133, 171
28:20........................... 71

MARK

1:11.............................. 168
9:2-13.......................... 168
14:62 171

LUKE

2:8-15........................... 32
2:52 57
16:19-31...................... 118
23:43 118
24:50-53 151

JOHN

1:1-3 34
1:14................2, 33, 35, 36
1:34 168
2:19-21......................... 127
3:1-15 164
5:22-27 151
5:22-29 118

5:25 118
5:26 166
8:58 60
10:1-21 129
10:14-18 94
10:16 154
11:17-27 148
11:35 6
11:44 127
12:1-8 130
12:20-21 155
12:24-25 155
12:32 155
14:9 35
14:16 132
14:18 132
14:18-24 149
14:23-30 132
15 166
16:5-7 163
16:7 133
16:8 164
17:3 60
19:25-27 130
20:1-10 127
20:11-15 128
20:16 128
20:17 130
20:18 131
20:19-23 131
20:22 132
20:24-27 134

ACTS

1:6-11 151
2:1-41 133
13:33 .... 167, 168
17:31 151
18:18-21 156
24:15 .... 118, 148

ROMANS

1:16 57
1:18-24 81
1:18-31 95
1:19-20 33
3:9-12 100

3:19 100
3:21-22 101
3:22b-23 102
3:24 103
3:25 103
3:26 107
3:30 72
4:25 138
5:1-11 145
5:12 .... 77, 78
5:12-14 80
5:12-21 .... 66, 77
5:13-14 80
6:1 90
6:1-14 146
6:12-13 90
6:14 91
8:3b 83
8:18-25 172
8:28-30 38

1 CORINTHIANS

1:28 34
2:1 57
8:6 60
12:13 165
15:12-49 118
15:18 139
15:20 148
15:25-26 171
15:20-28 66
15:35-49 152

2 CORINTHIANS

3:12–4:6 164
4:6 35
5:1-10 118
5:11-21 145
5:20 156
5:21 120
8:9 .... 47, 48

GALATIANS

2:20 86
5:22-25 166

EPHESIANS

1:3 165
1:13-14 165
2:3 11
2:4-6 11
2:17 .... 156, 157
2:18 165
4:8-10 118
5:25-28 94

PHILIPPIANS

2:4-8 .... 44, 45
2:7 .... 47, 48, 180, 193
2:8 76
2:9-11 118

COLOSSIANS

1:15-17 34
1:15-18 49
1:17b 49
1:18 .... 148, 172
1:20 174
2:9 2
2:13-15 115

1 THESSALONIANS

4:16 172
4:17 151

1 TIMOTHY

1:17 60
2:5 67
2:5-7 42

HEBREWS

1:1-3 .... 33, 49
1:3 .... 158, 160, 169
1:5 168
4:15 44
5:5 168
5:10 94
7:22 109
7:23-24 .... 109, 110
7:23-25 161
7:26-27 42

9:6-7............................ 110
9:7 159
9:11-14 160
9:15 95
10:11-12 109
10:12-14....................... 110
10:14 95
10:19-22....................... 146

James

2:19 60

1 Peter

1:8-9............................ 149
2:8 58
3:18 118

2 Peter

2:4 118

Revelation

5:8-10........................... 95
9:1-2 118
19:11-16 151
19–22:5........................ 172
20:11-15....................... 118
20:11-18....................... 148
21:1-4.......................... 173
21:8 148

Subject Index

A

Active obedience of Christ......... 83, 187
Allen, Michael 36, 37
Analogy 15, 25, 26, 97, 187
Apollinarianism................62, 64, 71, 72,
.... 73, 74, 181, 187
Aquinas, Thomas 34, 185
Arianism 74, 179, 188,
Ascension of Christ
    As completion of atonement 118-119
    Christ as Prophet 154-158
    Christ as Priest 158-163
    Christ as King.........................166-172
    Christ's return 171, 172
Athanasius 42, 43, 48, 74, 188
Atonement
    Holiness, love, and wrath 95
    Propitiation and substitution 99
    Definite atonement.........94, 109-110,
.... 111-115, 190
    Christus Victor.............. 115-117, 189
    Union with Christ.... 86, 89, 119, 121,
.... 146, 165, 196
Augustine.......................... 1, 29, 148, 149

B

Bavinck, Herman............................10, 33
Beauty of God
    Objectivity of beauty.................19-20
    Divine beauty and Trinity............. 50
    Divine accommodation 12
Butner, D. Glenn 58

C

Calvin, John 48
Chalcedon Definition............. 45-46, 63,
.... 66, 188
Christ
    Active obedience..............................83
    Passive obedience 83
    Impeccability........................... 85, 120
Christus Victor.................... 115-117, 189
Communicatio idiomatum ... 46, 69, 189
Covenant of Grace 189-190
Covenant of Redemption.... 28, 147, 190
Covenant of Works...................... 80, 190

D

Definite atonement............. 94, 109, 111,
.... 183, 190
Divine incomprehensibility 152
Divine simplicity.................... 96, 99, 182
Divine will 27, 38, 62, 75-76, 172,
.... 181, 182, 190
Dostoevsky, Fyodor 111
Dyothelitism............73, 74, 181, 190, 193

E

Edwards, Jonathan 122, 177
Eternal functional subordination ....
.... 182, 191
Eternal generation 132, 169, 191
Eternal processions.............. 29, 182, 191
Extra Calvinisticum...............48, 50, 192

F

Federal headship 78, 81, 192

G

Gregory of Nazianzus 86
Gregory of Nyssa.................................21

H

Hades 117-118
Heidelberg Catechism.................. 50, 51
Holy Spirit 29, 38, 121, 131,
.... 132, 133, 146, 149,
.... 154, 163, 164-166
Hypostatic union 45, 55, 58, 61,
.... 69, 85, 192

I

Immutability...........................98, 99, 192
Impassibility 193
Impeccability of Christ.................... 120
Incarnation
    Revealing God's nature.31-53, 69, 87
    Revealing God's work ..37-39, 58, 74,
....87, 137, 193
    Revealing human need 39-41
    Revealing divine provision 34,
.... 42-43, 170
Inseparable operations............27, 37, 38,
....104, 182, 193

J

Jamieson, R.B. 70
Justification....................81, 82, 103, 106,
....108, 138, 139, 193

K

Kenoticism 47, 180, 193
Kilby, Clyde... 24

L

Lewis, C.S...................................... 4, 16, 24
Luther, Martin......................116-117, 119

M

Markos, Louis..4
Maximus the Confessor.......................76
Milton, John................................. 137-138
Monothelitism.........73, 74, 181, 190, 193

N

Nestorianism 62, 65, 66, 181, 193
Nicene Creed 27, 34, 35, 77, 173, 194

O

Omnipotence................................ 12, 194
Omnipresence 12, 50, 69, 194
Omniscience 12, 194

P

Parousia.. 172, 194
Partitive exegesis................... 70, 71, 194
Passive obedience of Christ......... 83, 90,
.... 121, 194
Penal substitutionary atonement 188
Platonism 15, 195
Propitiation................. 99, 103-104, 105,
.... 106, 107, 115, 159, 195

R

Recapitulation 82, 137, 195
Resurrection of Christ
    Narrative in John's Gospel ... 127-137
    Theological significance 83, 115,
.... 118, 126-150,
.... 167, 168, 170
    Assurance and forgiveness......67, 83,
....118
    Union with Christ......... 121, 123, 130
Revelation..................................... 172, 196

S

Sanders, Fred 35-36
Schreiner, Patrick....................... 154, 167
Scripture, illumination of.......... 2, 3, 24,
.... 164, 178, 194, 196
Shakespeare, William 140, 144
Sin, conviction of................................. 30

T

Theotokos....................................65, 66, 67
Tolkien, J.R.R....................................... 126
Trinity
    Divine beauty 3, 5, 10-12, 31,
.................................50, 52-53, 174
        Revelation in incarnation....6, 33-39,
....40, 42, 47, 50,
.... 52, 170, 178
        Historical development of doctrine..
....58-65, 99, 182, 193
Turretin, Francis.............................87, 88

U

Union with Christ......... 86, 89, 119, 121,
.... 146, 165, 196
Ursinus, Zacharias............................... 50

W

Wax, Trevin 72
Wesley, Charles 162
Williams, Niall............................ 113-114
Wittman, Tyler R. 70

Also available from Christian Focus Publications ...

IRRESISTIBLE
BEAUTY

BEHOLDING TRIUNE GLORY
IN THE FACE OF JESUS CHRIST

SAMUEL G. PARKISON

SERIES EDITORS J.V. FESKO & MATTHEW BARRETT

978-1-5271-0914-8

IRRESISTIBLE BEAUTY

Beholding Triune Glory in the Face of Jesus Christ

SAMUEL G. PARKISON

In this doxologically flavored, dogmatically charged work, Parkison pulls from a variety of disciplines to demonstrate Christ's beauty, and the relevance of Christ's beauty on Christian theology. Irresistible Beauty is the work of a synthetic generalist. It is not strictly a work of exegesis, though it will stand firmly on exegetical findings. It is not strictly a work of biblical theology, though it will be biblical–theological. It is not strictly a work of historical theology, though it will engage in theological retrieval of the church's history. It is not strictly a philosophical work, though, driven by a love for wisdom, it will be irreducibly philosophical. Thus, this is a systematic–theological work in the full sense of the term—informed and shaped by these disciplines and informing and shaping the pursuit of them.

… a compelling biblical case for retrieving the glorious beauty of the truth and goodness of the good news of Jesus Christ. 'Irresistible Beauty' is an important argument for appreciating the aesthetic dimension of saving faith.

KEVIN J. VANHOOZER
Trinity Evangelical Divinity School,
Deerfield, Illinois

Christian Focus Publications

Our mission statement
Staying Faithful

In dependence upon God we seek to impact the world through literature faithful to His infallible Word, the Bible. Our aim is to ensure that the Lord Jesus Christ is presented as the only hope to obtain forgiveness of sin, live a useful life and look forward to heaven with Him.

Our Books are published in four imprints:

◁◯✕ CHRISTIAN FOCUS

Popular works including biographies, commentaries, basic doctrine and Christian living.

◁◯✕ MENTOR

Books written at a level suitable for Bible College and seminary students, pastors, and other serious readers. The imprint includes commentaries, doctrinal studies, examination of current issues and church history.

◁◯✕ CHRISTIAN HERITAGE

Books representing some of the best material from the rich heritage of the church.

◁◯✕ CF4KIDS

Children's books for quality Bible teaching and for all age groups: Sunday school curriculum, puzzle and activity books; personal and family devotional titles, biographies and inspirational stories – because you are never too young to know Jesus!

Christian Focus Publications Ltd,
Geanies House, Fearn, Ross-shire,
IV20 1TW, Scotland, United Kingdom.
www.christianfocus.com